SPIRITUAL DISCIPLINES WITHIN THE CHURCH

SPIRITUAL DISCIPLINES WITHIN THE CHURCH

Participating Fully in the Body of Christ

DONALD S. WHITNEY

FOREWORD BY
JAMES M. BOICE

ISBN: 0–8024–7746–1

7 9 10 8

Printed in the United States of America

For our holy, gracious, and loving triune God.
"To Him be *glory in the church* by Christ Jesus
to all generations, forever and ever.
Amen."
Ephesians 3:21

And for reformation and revival
in the church
in our time.
Amen.

CONTENTS

. . . . ⚜ . . . .

FOREWORD

. . . . ⚜ . . . .

In the last twenty years something terrible has happened to Americans. They no longer relate to other people or care about them—at least not very much. Instead the majority focus on themselves and deal with others only for what they can get out of them.

In 1981 a sociologist-pollster, Daniel Yankelovich, published a study of the 1970s titled *New Rules: Searching for Self-Fulfillment in a World Turned Upside Down.* This book documented a tidal shift in values by which many and eventually most Americans began to seek personal self-fulfillment as the ultimate goal in life rather than operating on the principle that we are here to serve and even sacrifice for others, as Americans for the most part had done previously. Yankelovich found that by the late 1970s, 72 percent of Americans spent much time thinking about themselves and their inner lives. So pervasive was this change that as early as 1976 Tom Wolfe called the seventies the "Me Decade" and compared it to a third religious awakening.

Some awakening! More like the death of community!

In his best-selling book *The Greening of America,* Charles Reich wrote, "Modern living has obliterated place, locality and neighborhood, and given us the anonymous separateness of our existence. The family, the most basic social system, has been ruthlessly stripped to its functional essentials. Friendship has been coated over with a layer of impenetrable artificiality as men strive to live roles designed for them. Protocol, competition, hostility and fear have replaced the warmth of the circle of affection which might sustain man against a hostile environment." He said that "America [has become] one vast, terrifying anti-community."

It wasn't meant to be this way, of course. At the very beginning of human history, God created a woman for the man, saying, "It is not good for the man to be alone" (Genesis 2:18 NASB). Then, two thousand

9

years ago in Palestine Jesus Christ said, "I will build My church" (Matthew 16:18). He did not come merely to call individuals to salvation. He came to build a church. Christians are created to be that church and community.

Don Whitney understands this well and is disturbed at how our present sad individualism has impacted the church and people's view of it. He pastored Glenfield Baptist Church in Glen Ellyn, Illinois, for more than fourteen years and knows the questions that even Christian people ask: Why go to church? Why join a particular church? What can I gain by the church's services or ceremonies? By baptism or even preaching? Why should I give money to the church? Can't I do just fine by myself? As a woman named Sheila once said to Robert Bellah, author of *Habits of the Heart,* "I have my own religion. I call it Sheilaism, just my own little voice."

It is these questions that Whitney answers in this volume, and the answers he gives are ones I heartily recommend to you. They are easy to read, but they commend a good reading and thoughtful reflection too.

Maybe they will be heard and followed and we can get back to the strong kind of church described for us in the book of Acts. We read there that the early Christians "devoted themselves to the apostles' teaching and to the fellowship, to the breaking of bread and to prayer. . . . Every day they continued to meet together in the temple courts. They broke bread in their homes and ate together with glad and sincere hearts, praising God and enjoying the favor of all the people" (Acts 2:42, 46–47 NASB).

This was truly an example of the new humanity, the very thing the world needed then and desperately needs again. No wonder the chapter concludes by noting, "And the Lord added to their number daily those who were being saved" (v. 47 NASB). God blesses when those who are called by His name obey Him.

JAMES MONTGOMERY BOICE

ACKNOWLEDGMENTS

· · · · · · · ❖ · · · · · · ·

I love baseball. In the baseball-filled summers of my youth I enjoyed nothing more than swinging a slender cylinder of white ash (these were the days just before the advent of aluminum bats) and trying to crack a fastball off the brick of the old school building in deep centerfield at Hale Field in Osceola, Arkansas. When I was standing at the plate and the pitcher wound up and threw one belt-high, no one could swing the bat for me. And yet, in another sense, I was there as part of a team.

As I sat hour after hour at the computer, no one could write this book for me. And yet, there was a team of people supporting me in my writing, and without them you wouldn't be reading these words now. On this page I want to thank them publicly.

Thanks, Jim Bell, for contacting me and for believing in the need for this book. I hope you enjoy the Stan Musial picture. Thanks to Cheryl Dunlop, and to all at Moody Press for your patience for all the "time-outs" that made this a very long at-bat.

Thanks, Glenfield Baptist Church in Glen Ellyn, Illinois. Tears fill my eyes as I type these words and think of you. What a wonderful fourteen-and-a-half years we had together. So much of this book is from you and for you. Thanks for all the prayers and loving encouragement to help me to finish this book.

Thanks, new colleagues at Midwestern Baptist Theological Seminary in Kansas City, Missouri. You have stimulated me in so many ways during the final six months of this project. Thanks for listening, advising, and cheering me on.

Thanks, all my family and friends who prayed and helped me persevere in writing while going through one of the most prolonged upheavals in my life.

Thank you, Caffy and Laurelen, for loving me through it all. You are infinitely more important to me than this book.

Thank You, Lord, for the grace over all, for the health and strength, and for the words that I thought would never come. All the glory for this book is Yours. May You be pleased to use this volume as an instrument for reformation and revival in Your church.

INTRODUCTION

· · · · · · · · ✤ · · · · · · · · ·

W hy did I write this book?

I wrote this book *to declare the glory of the church and to invite people to enjoy the church.* Jesus Christ is the glory of the church. He loves the church and died for the church (Acts 20:28; Ephesians 5:25). With all of its spots and wrinkles, He is at work in and through the church. Regardless of how you view the general condition of the church today or the state of the individual churches in your area, the ultimate future of the church is glorious beyond imagination. Therefore the potential for joy is greater in the church than is promised to any other earthly entity. As the local church is still comprised of sinners in a fallen world, there's no denying the reality of failure and discord in the church. But with all its faults, because of Christ there is more to enjoy in the church than the world dreams of.

I also wrote it *to contend against the consumeristic view of the church prevalent today.* The church of Jesus Christ is increasingly being viewed as a religious shopping mall. Many who attend do so as religious consumers who feel no more sense of commitment to the church than does a consumer to a mall. As with marketplace consumers to a mall, religious consumers perceive no responsibility to the church except (perhaps) to give money in exchange for services rendered. The problem with this attitude (besides the main problem, that it is contrary to biblical Christianity) is that it is self-defeating. A church that has decreasing numbers of people willing to serve in its ministries will have fewer ministries to offer to consumers.

And I penned these pages *to contend against the privatization of spirituality.* The current interest in spirituality and the Spiritual Disciplines too often manifests itself in a privatized Christianity. Spirituality is seldom considered in the context of the church body. But the personal Spiritual Disciplines (the subject of my *Spiritual Disciplines for the Christian Life,* NavPress, 1991) are not intended to make us spiritually self-absorbed evangelical monks. The church is a community in which Christians are to live and experience much of their Christianity. Too many believers isolate themselves from life with the family of God, deceived by the notion that "me and Jesus" are all they need in order to be all that God wants them to become and to savor all He has for them. Such individualization of the faith hurts the church. What too few see is that anything that hurts the church eventually hurts them as individual Christians.

Additionally, I wrote this book *to encourage those who love the church.* The world is well-salted with saints who love the church and are burdened for its renewal. Pastors everywhere are concerned about the increasingly common lack of commitment to the church, not only by nominal Christians, but among supposedly mature believers. Faithful church members are discouraged by the new beliefs and practices of their ministers, which are anesthetizing the congregation. I want them to take heart about the future of the church. I also want to furnish them with a resource for strengthening their own church.

Moreover, I developed this volume *to help growing Christians learn about the church.* If Jesus Christ died for the church, then it's worth our time to find out what *our* responsibility is to the church. Many of the subjects covered here will not be new to those who are regular churchgoers. However, upon reflection you may realize that you don't know *why* you should do these things, other than that they are traditional (and perhaps outdated?) aspects of church life. This book will not only give you biblical reasons for these practices, but also provide some workable insights and helpful suggestions for doing them.

Finally, I composed *Spiritual Disciplines Within the Church* for *anyone interested in spirituality.* Some may pick up this book because of their attraction to the subject of spirituality, finding the title intriguing since it approaches the matter from a different angle than they are accustomed to. Others may open these pages because they've been thinking about attending church for the first time or returning after a long absence. Here you'll find a presentation of the Bible's teaching that true spirituality is found in knowing God through Jesus Christ and in becoming like Christ, and that becoming like Christ means loving His church.

CHAPTER ONE

WHY GO TO CHURCH?

. . . . ❧ . . . .

I was glad when they said to me,
"Let us go into the house of the Lord."
Psalm 122:1

Why should I read anything about going to church?

That's a fair question since the odds are extremely high that you *do* go to church—otherwise you probably wouldn't be reading this book. But here's why even the most faithful churchgoer should know what's in this chapter.

First, if God has spoken in the Bible about going to church, then His Word on this matter deserves to be proclaimed faithfully and to be received reverently.

Second, those of us who attend church need to evaluate our reasons and make sure that our basis for going is not habit alone. Do you go to church for biblical reasons? Do you *know* the biblical reasons? We've all heard that we should go to church, but have you ever heard that appeal based upon Scripture?

Third, church attendance may be a settled matter for many Christian adults reading this, but your children may not be convinced that going to church is for them. So although *you* may not need persuading in this matter, the information in this chapter can be useful for you in talking to them.

Fourth, some who are reading these words attend church only occasionally. A survey conducted in 1991 reported that one of every eight people who describe themselves as "born-again Christians" do not go to church.[1] Anyone who claims to follow Christ but seldom, if ever, attends His church needs to be challenged with what the Bible says about going to church.

Fifth, there may be others turning these pages who are thinking about giving up on church altogether. Even though you may have been faithful in church for a long time, you are no longer sure about continuing. You, too, need the biblical challenge and reasoning to stay in church.

Did you go to church last Sunday? If you did, you are in the minority of Americans. Although America has one of the highest percentages of churchgoers of any nation, more than half the people in this country did not go to church this past Lord's Day.

Ask why people don't attend church, and you'll get a variety of responses, but most of them fall into about a dozen categories. Some say they don't go to church because they are turned off by what seems an endless asking for money. Others stay away because church services bore them. A percentage of those who have no interest in church say the sermons are irrelevant to their lives. Some refuse to go because when they do attend they leave feeling guilty.

Numbers of people stay home because Sunday is their only day off and they want to spend it doing other things. On the other hand, some can't be at church because they are working. Additionally, there are always those who are absent from church because of bad experiences with churches in the past. Many say that the only reason they do not go is that they have not been invited, and they would feel uncomfortable going alone.

A few stay away because they think their lifestyle is too unacceptable to the expectations of churchgoers. A lot of folks are convinced the church simply has nothing to offer them. Similarly, many admit that they don't have enough interest in religion to attend church. And one of the most common reasons given why people don't go to church is that there just isn't time.

It doesn't take all twelve of these arguments to keep someone from church. Usually *one* of them weighs heavily enough on the scales of a person's judgment to decide the issue. But even for the believer who is persuaded by one of these, with the happiness of this life and all eternity at stake, it's worth considering what the Bible has to say on the other side of the matter.

Here are twelve biblical reasons for going to church.

GOING TO CHURCH IS A BIBLICAL
REQUIREMENT FOR ALL CHRISTIANS

A recent major survey of a cross section of Americans shows that almost half (47 percent) agree that "the Bible does not command people to attend a church; that is a man-made requirement."[2] In fact, the Bible is very plain: "And let us consider one another in order to stir up love and good works, *not forsaking the assembling of ourselves together, as is the manner of some,* but exhorting one another, and so much the more as you see the Day approaching" (Hebrews 10:24–25, italics added).

Referring to the public meeting of the church body, this verse clearly tells believers not to forsake the regular assembly of fellow Christians, but rather to go to church.

This command wasn't given whimsically. The author recognized what these Jewish Christians were facing. In their place and time, to identify themselves openly (as through church attendance) with other followers of Christ meant persecution, the seizure of property, and possibly imprisonment (Hebrews 10:34). But the inspired writer of this letter knew that more important than those potential losses were the certain benefits gained through gathering with God's faithful.

If this chapter ended here, no further proof would be needed concerning God's will about church attendance. God has spoken in this passage about the matter, and the issue should be settled. Ultimately, whether or not you go to church is a question of whether you will obey God and submit to the authority of His Word.

Do you profess to be a Christian? It is dangerously deceptive to think, "as is the manner of some," that you can get the salvation and security of heaven you need through the message of the church and then withdraw, "forsaking the assembling" of the fellowship. The church is not a department store where you come and get the spiritual commodity you want, then go your way. To speak of loving Christ while neglecting His body, the church (Ephesians 1:23; 4:12, 15–16; 5:29–30), is hypocritical.

GOING TO CHURCH HELPS PREVENT
BACKSLIDING AND APOSTASY

The great concern of the writer of Hebrews 10:25 was that a spiritual erosion was taking place within those who had gotten into the habit of neglecting the meetings of the church. He knew that if they continued to shun the public worship of God with the people of God they would be in danger of spiritual ruin.

Neglect of church attendance is almost always one of the first outward signs of backsliding and one of the initial steps taken by those whose path ends in complete apostasy. Statistics show that if you don't go to church for a month, the odds are almost two-to-one that you won't go for more than a year.[3] Without the encouragement to persevere that is provided by the public worship of God, the preaching of the Word of God, and the fellowship of the people of God, there is a much greater tendency to drift spiritually.

A couple in our church recently told me how several years of infrequent church attendance had withered their spiritual lives. A family tragedy prompted them to return to faithfulness. Once back in church, a spiritual snowball effect has happened. Their personal devotional lives, family relationships, service for the Lord, and more have all experienced renewal as by-products of the biblical exhortation and Christian encouragement they've received by returning to active involvement with the church family.

Of course, church attendance is no automatic guarantee against spiritual setbacks. No Christian progresses in faith with perfect consistency. But without going to church, backsliding—or worse—is almost a certainty. In fact, based upon Hebrews 10:25, "forsaking the assembling of ourselves together" actually *is* backsliding. If you can miss church and not *miss* church, then something is absent from your heart and faith.

GOING TO CHURCH BRINGS SPIRITUAL
FELLOWSHIP AND ENCOURAGEMENT

A summary of the regular activities of the first-ever Christian church (which was in Jerusalem) is recorded in Acts 2:42: "And they continued steadfastly in the apostles' doctrine and fellowship, in the breaking of bread, and in prayers." This verse tells us that one of the four main characteristics of the church's gatherings was " fellowship."

In Hebrews 10:25 again, when we're told, "Let us not give up meeting together," the desired contrasting response is "but let us encourage one another" (NIV). No Christian can thrive without the two spiritual nutrients mentioned here of *fellowship* and *encouragement*. God has made us to need them. And it is also God's plan for us to receive most of our fellowship and encouragement from the local church family.

Fellowship is more than socializing; it is qualitatively different. Any two people can socialize. Only Christians can fellowship, at least in the biblical sense. Socializing is a gift from God. It is the setting where fellowship happens; nevertheless, fellowship exceeds socializing in beauty and enjoyment as does spring's tulip over winter's bulb.

New Testament fellowship involves the sharing of the Christian life with other followers of Christ. Talking about the things of God with each other, telling and hearing testimonies of the work of the Spirit of God in our lives, serving the Lord and His people together, worshiping God and praying as one people, extending to and receiving from one another the love of Christ—these are the fibers of the fabric of fellowship. The best way for it to be woven into our lives is through involvement with a church family.

When we go to church, we can receive encouragement from the preaching and the teaching of God's Word (see Romans 15:4–5). We can be encouraged by the perseverance of other believers who are buoyant in their faith despite discouraging circumstances, by the example of more mature believers, by other church members who struggle successfully with some of the same daily issues we face, and by praying and singing the praises of God with others.

If a child is going to be emotionally healthy, he needs the socialization and encouragement a family can provide. In the same way, every child of God needs the fellowship and encouragement that God intends for him to receive from a church family if he is going to be spiritually healthy.

GOING TO CHURCH EXPRESSES OBEDIENCE
TO THE GREATEST COMMANDMENT

In Mark 12:28–30, a man asked Jesus, " 'Which is the first commandment of all?' And Jesus answered him, 'The first of all the commandments is: "Hear, O Israel, the Lord our God, the Lord is one. And you shall love the Lord your God with all your heart, with all your soul, with all your mind, and with all your strength." This is the first commandment.'"

How can we believe we're trying to fulfill the greatest of all God's commandments, and how can we say we want to love the Lord our God with all that we are, if we won't even obey His command to meet regularly with other Christians? How can we say that we love Him with everything that's in us if we can't get out of bed to worship Him with His people?

Is God your greatest love and highest priority? Going to church is one way of demonstrating that. A quick, unreluctant willingness to turn your back on the worship of God in order to work, attend ballgames (including children's ballgames), entertain guests, participate in recreational sports, and so forth, may indicate to family, friends, and others that God really is not your first love. Or it may indicate that you are willing to let those who do not love God or care about His kingdom's activities determine your priorities, set your schedule, and keep you from the worship and work of God.

In high school I played four sports. My parents came to every game in every sport, no matter how inconvenient the timing or how far the drive, *except* the out-of-town Sunday baseball games that were scheduled at a time requiring that they miss church. Because they came to all other games, I knew they loved me. But because they didn't come to the ones that conflicted with the worship of God, I knew they loved Him more than they loved me, and that was critical for me to know and see.

Francois Fénelon was the court preacher for King Louis XIV of France in the 1600s. One Sunday the king and his attendants made their grand entrance into the chapel, only to discover that no one else was there.

"What does this mean?" King Louis demanded.

"I had published that you would not be here today," Fénelon replied, "in order that Your Majesty might see who serves God in truth and who flatters the king." [4]

We should go to church because we love God more than anyone or anything else.

GOING TO CHURCH FOLLOWS JESUS' EXAMPLE

Do you want to be like Jesus? Do you realize that Jesus made it

His regular practice to attend the public worship of God the Father with the people of God?

The Bible tells us in Luke 4:16, "And as His custom was, He went into the synagogue on the Sabbath day . . ." Granted, Jesus was participating in the *Jewish* worship of God, but it was the way God had ordained worship at the time. The principle remains the same: If we are to be like Jesus, then like Him we will attend the public worship of God as ordained by God for our day, along with others who want to obey God and be like Jesus.

Many people who don't go to church object that they have many other things to do. Yet the people who are the most faithful in church attendance have as much to do as anyone else. Everyone *always* has *something* that needs to be done at home, at school, at work, in the yard, with the car, with the children, etc. If people came to church only when they had nothing else to do, most churches would be empty on Sundays!

But considering Jesus' example of attending public worship eliminates the excuse of being too busy for church. Jesus also had countless crucial things He could have been doing rather than attending worship. He even had *spiritual* and *eternal* reasons He could have given for not having time for corporate worship. Jesus had the kingdom of God to build, many people to change, needs to meet, diseases to heal, and numberless other demands upon His time. People by the thousands were almost always clamoring for His attention, pleading for His mercy, begging for His help, and crying for Him to heal them. And yet, Jesus refused to let these incessant and very important supplications keep Him from attending public worship. He did not use this daily, unrelenting job stress as an excuse to avoid crowds and to stay away from the group of people gathered to worship God.

If Jesus believed that participating in public worship was that important, so should we.

GOING TO CHURCH IS A TESTIMONY OF
SUPPORT FOR GOD'S WORK IN THE WORLD

Jesus taught this by implication when He said in Matthew 12:30, "He who is not with Me is against Me, and he who does not gather with Me scatters abroad."

Are you with Christ or against Him? Are you with Him in gathering people into His family—the church—or are you scattering people from Him? Jesus allows for only two kinds of people in this statement. Each of us is either with Him as a gatherer or against Him as a scatterer.

"I'm not against You, Jesus!" many nonattenders would protest. But the example of their lives denies their professed loyalty. The work of the church is the work of gathering. Going to church testifies that you support such work. When you stay away, you not only fail to support this work of gathering, you actually work against it like a scatterer. You scatter those such as your family and friends who might be gathered under the influence of Christ's work if you attended church.

"I don't have to go to church to show that I support Christ's work!" comes the objection. "I give to Christian causes and do Christian service." But people know where you go Sunday morning. They see you going to church while they are out exercising, gardening, or getting their newspapers. They see by this what's important to you and that you are committed to the support of God's work in this world. This is part of the work of gathering. Staying away from church does not help gather people to Jesus.

GOING TO CHURCH ENABLES YOU TO HEAR
IN PERSON THE PREACHING OF GOD'S WORD

God has ordained preaching. To those He has called to this ministry He gives the command: "Preach the word! Be ready in season and out of season. Convince, rebuke, exhort, with all longsuffering and teaching. For the time will come when they will not endure sound doctrine, but according to their own desires, because they have itching ears, they will heap up for themselves teachers; and they will turn their ears away from the truth, and be turned aside to fables" (2 Timothy 4:2–4).

Since God commanded that His Word be preached, then He means for the preached Word to be heard. Going to church is the best way to listen to the preaching of God's Word.

"But," someone objects, "I can hear God's Word preached just as well on radio or television or tapes!"

Yes, Christians (as well as non-Christians) who are unable to attend church can experience the proclamation of the truth of God when they might have missed it otherwise. Through such ministries many Christians find additional edification to supplement the preaching and teaching they hear in church.

However, there are many reasons why no Christian should substitute a media ministry for attendance at, and participation in, a local church. (Of course, if a person is physically unable to attend church, that is a different matter.) We have room here to consider only a few reasons that listening to preaching in person is preferable to any other method of hearing God's Word.

For one thing, inherent in the convenience of media preaching is the ability to turn it off if the message becomes too uncomfortable or "uninteresting." The ease with which the channel may be changed to a more pleasing or entertaining speaker also increases the temptation for people to "gather around them a great number of teachers to say what their itching ears want to hear" (2 Timothy 4:3 NIV) and to "turn their ears away from the truth" (v. 4). Sometimes what is uncomfortable or what seems at first uninteresting proves to be exactly what we need to hear. When we control the messenger and thus the message, we often miss that which God would have us hear, but which we would never choose.

Another problem with not hearing preaching in person is that the sense of immediacy is absent in media preaching. There is a dynamic element in preaching that simply cannot be communicated through the media. Think, for instance, of the difference between hearing your fiancé say "I love you" on videotape and hearing the same message in person.

A third difficulty with substituting media ministry for church attendance is the inevitable individualization it fosters. The more accustomed you grow to sermon-tasting with your remote control, the more satisfied you become with this kind of fast-food, have-it-your-way Christianity.

Theologian and former editor of *Christianity Today* Kenneth Kantzer has observed that watching church instead of attending "tends not only to breed disloyalty to the church but to foster an isolated, private, and individualistic kind of Christianity; and that is not the kind of Christianity nourished in the Bible."[5]

I should mention here one underlying assumption that relates not only to this point, but to the whole idea of attending church. *Make sure that the church you attend believes the Bible, and that in the preaching and teaching of the church the Bible is openly emphasized.* (I will deal with this further in the last chapter.)

The Bible exhorts the children of God in 1 Peter 2:2, "As new-born babes, desire the pure milk of the word, that you may grow thereby." Christians should desire more of God's Word than they get in preaching at church, but they should at least desire it enough to want to come for it at church. I can understand the Christian who can't get enough of the Word from the sermons at church, but not the one who gets enough without church.

GOING TO CHURCH ALLOWS YOU
TO TAKE THE LORD'S SUPPER

Jesus Himself said concerning the Lord's Supper, "Do this in remembrance of Me" (Luke 22:19). It is the will of God, made clear by direct command, that we are to participate in the Lord's Supper, or Communion.

The Lord's Supper was given to the *church* for observance, not to individual Christians. This is an ordinance of Christ that should be celebrated in the fellowship of a local church. Thus it is by attendance at the setting where the Lord's Supper is offered that we can obey the Lord and share in this memorial to Him.

The apostle Paul said of this special event, "For as often as you eat this bread and drink this cup, you proclaim the Lord's death till He comes" (1 Corinthians 11:26). Surely taking the Lord's Supper, and thereby proclaiming the death of the Lord, is not something a true Christian would want to do infrequently, much less ignore altogether. Does any Christian want to say, "I don't care to proclaim the death of Christ; I don't care to participate in the memorial of what Jesus has done for me"? That's exactly what we do if we do not go to church.

GOING TO CHURCH ENABLES YOU TO
EXPERIENCE SPECIAL BLESSINGS FROM GOD

Although it's true that there are spiritual experiences God gives only in private worship, it is also true that, despite the depth of your personal devotional life, there are blessings the Father gives only in the context of *public* worship.

That's illustrated in the following two verses in which Paul describes something of the worship of God in a particular church: "Whenever you come together, each of you has a psalm, has a teaching, has a tongue, has a revelation, has an interpretation. Let all things be done for edification. . . . For you can all prophesy one by one, that all may learn and all may be encouraged" (1 Corinthians 14:26, 31).

Although there may be some disagreement about the meaning of several things in this passage, this much is clear: all these things could not have happened in an individual's *private* worship. Paul reminds these Christians that this spiritual "edification" or strengthening and the benefits that come when "all may learn and all may be encouraged" occur only "whenever you come together."

The same is still true for us as well. In ways that He does not do when we worship Him alone, God blesses us with strength, instruction, and encouragement when we come together at church to worship Him.

GOING TO CHURCH HELPS PREVENT AN UNBALANCED CHRISTIAN LIFE

Christians who do not attend church are usually the most unbalanced Christians. The difficulty, however, is that they don't realize it. It's not easy to discern when your Christian life is unbalanced. Others can usually detect a lack of balance in us better than we can see it in ourselves. That's another reason it's crucial for us to attend church. The Lord uses His body, the church, to protect us against the common temptations that lead to imbalance.

In Ephesians 4:11–16, we're told that God gives gifted individuals to the church to equip and strengthen it. One result of their work is a more healthy spiritual balance for those in the church, as described in verse 14: "That we should no longer be children, tossed to and fro and carried about with every wind of doctrine, by the trickery of men, in the cunning craftiness of deceitful plotting."

Those who are not an active part of a local church body are much more susceptible to being blown back and forth by spiritual fads. Apart from the care and discernment of a family of believers, they become easier targets for teachers who have no doctrinal accountability.

In a local church, not only are ministry leaders shepherding the flock, there is also the added protection of fellowship with other members. Fellow church members have spiritual gifts and insights you do not have. Other members may spot doctrinal error or a tendency to be unbalanced in priorities when you do not see it. Furthermore, they can provide ready counsel when you encounter questionable teaching from books, radio, or other ministries outside the church.

Ephesians 4:16 speaks of Christ—"from whom the whole body, joined and knit together by what every joint supplies, according to the effective working by which every part does its share, causes growth of the body for the edifying of itself in love." Notice that this growth, which is stable and balanced, happens as "every part does its share." If you aren't a "part" of a church body, it's unlikely that this balanced spiritual growth will happen for you.

GOING TO CHURCH IS ONE
INDICATION OF ETERNAL LIFE

Church attendance is not *proof* that a person has eternal life, but it is one favorable indication. First John 3:14 leads us to believe that those with eternal life will want to go to church. That verse says, "We know that we have passed from death to life, because we love the brethren."

In other words, one way we can know we have passed out of spiritual death into spiritual life, and one way we can confirm we have the eternal life of a Christian, is that we possess a new, active love for our brothers and sisters in Jesus. We discover in ourselves a God-given love for them that's more cohesive than that which we have for those who are not Christians.

How can anyone say he has this kind of heaven-generated love for the "brethren" when he doesn't even love them enough to be with them? How can anyone who truly has this love for the family of God have no desire to gather with his brothers and sisters at the "family reunions" each Sunday when they meet with their Father?

Can you imagine any person affirming his love for his family, but then saying that he doesn't care if he ever sees them again? Such "love" is a contradiction in terms. But that is the kind of "love" many professing Christians demonstrate for their spiritual family.

Those who "have passed from death to life" are compelled by a oneness with others who have eternal life. They are one in their love for God, one in their love for His Word and work, one in their worship of Him, one in their purposes. And they do not want to stay away when the others gather together.

NOT GOING TO CHURCH IS ONE
INDICATION OF *NOT* BEING IN GOD'S FAMILY

While church attendance typically characterizes Christians, people who aren't interested in going to church may have that attitude precisely because they are *not* Christians.

I make such a bold statement based upon God's Word in 1 John 2:19. In this verse, the apostle John clarifies for his readers why some people had stopped being a part of their fellowship. "They went out from us," he explains, "but they were not of us; for if they had been of us, they would have continued with us; but they went out that they might be made manifest, that none of them were of us." If they really belonged to the Christian family, John reasons, they would show it by their presence with the family. Their absence reveals the spurious nature of their Christianity.

Anyone who, without regret, is persistently willing to disobey the Lord's command to meet with the people of God when they gather for public worship (Hebrews 10:25), and who is willing to forsake all the privileges and blessings God provides through the local church, may have some "religion," but he or she does not have biblical Christianity.

OTHER CONSIDERATIONS
REGARDING CHURCH ATTENDANCE

Going to church does not make you a Christian.

You must know Jesus Christ, the Head of the church, through repentance and faith in order to be right with God. Church attendance does not gain favor with God. There are many in hell who went to church all their lives. Regular church attendance is meaningless without a personal relationship with Jesus Christ, who is the Head of the church (Ephesians 4:15).

Until we know Jesus, our sin separates us from God (Isaiah 59:2; Romans 3:23) and leaves us "having no hope and without God in the world" (Ephesians 2:12) and unprepared to stand before God at the Judgment (Hebrews 9:27).

Here's why knowing Christ is so crucial. It is His sacrificial death as a willing substitute for the sins of others that makes believers in Him to be right with God (2 Corinthians 5:21; 1 Peter 3:18). The appropriate response by us to the work of Christ is, according to Jesus, to "repent, and believe in the gospel" (Mark 1:15).

To repent involves a change of mind toward God that results in a change of life. Repentance means to turn from loving yourself more than God, and to turn from living for yourself more than for God. Genuine repentance is expressed in a new love for God, a new affection for the things of God, and a new desire for obedience to God and His Word.

To believe is to trust Jesus Christ and His work to make you right with God. It involves faith that God will forgive your sins and accept you forever, not because of any work you have done, but on the basis of what Jesus alone has done. Biblical belief also includes the confidence that Jesus' resurrection from the dead is the evidence that all that Jesus did and said is true and from God.

Have you repented and believed biblically?

Make sure that the church you attend believes and proclaims this message; otherwise, your attendance there is a waste of time.

Going to church is vital for Christians.

Some people think of going to church the way they think of taking bad-tasting, but necessary, medicine. Instead, we need to view God's will about being at church as an expression of His kindness and care. The "church experience" is good for us and needed by us, or our loving Father wouldn't have stressed it so strongly and promised so much grace through it.

Every command of God is a law of love. He tells us to congregate with Christians because He intends to strengthen and bless us lovingly through one another. Sometimes homeless people refuse offers of care and protection by good people only because a long, familiar loneliness is preferable to the strangeness of family love. They cannot see how much they really lose because of what they imagine they would lose in giving up their rootlessness. Some "homeless" Christians think the same way. However, there is no benefit, real or imagined, in alienation from the body of Christ.

Not going to church is self-centered and foolish.

This is based upon Proverbs 18:1: "A man who isolates himself seeks his own desire; he rages against all wise judgment."

The person who isolates himself from church involvement conveys that he's self-centered rather than God-centered. He obviously isn't making his reclusive choice based upon the teaching of Philippians 2:3–4: "Do nothing from selfishness or empty conceit, but with humility of mind let each of you regard one another as more important than himself; do not merely look out for your own personal interests, but also for the interests of others" (NASB). We don't go to church merely for what it does for us, but also as a ministry to others.

And it's not wise judgment, but foolish pride which makes a person think, "I don't need those people at church." It's pride that says, "I don't need what all other believers need. *They* may need worship and preaching and corporate prayer, but I don't." There also can be a bit of spiritual snobbery involved, as though the person has a private connection to God that other believers lack.

Such isolation is also a failure to love, a selfish individualism demonstrated by the habit of some who neglect meeting together as God has ordained. This is true even if you are worshiping God at home while others are at public worship. Your exclusionist worship only proves the proverb: "A man who isolates himself seeks his own desire." You may be building yourself up as you are worshiping alone, but you could also be encouraging others and the preacher by your presence, words, and actions if you were worshiping God with them. If private worship were sufficient, God wouldn't have commanded public worship.

Not going to church is willful disobedience to the authority of God.

Regardless of feelings and reasons to stay away, we must face the fact that avoiding church is a willful repudiation of the authority of God, who explicitly commands us not to forsake the public assembly of believers (Hebrews 10:25). When God says to draw near to Him with His people, we disown both Him and His family when we refuse to come.

No church will be perfect or free from offensive things.

Because they are comprised of people, even the best churches have times when they do not live up to what they profess. Those who dwell on the imperfections of churches can convince themselves that the "organized church" is unworthy of their support. The best families have problems, too, but the benefits of being part of a good family with problems are much preferable to the handful of hollow advantages of having no family at all. True, you don't have to look long or hard to find valid criticisms of any church. But mature thinkers realize this and love God's church anyway. That's because they know that, with all its flaws, God still loves the church.

As the apostle Paul asked in 1 Corinthians 11:22, "Do you despise the church of God?" If not, will you commit yourself to attend the services of your church faithfully?

CHAPTER TWO

WHY SEEK BAPTISM IN THE CHURCH?

. . . . ✦ . . . .

*Evangelicals need to affirm aggressively the necessary
connection between faith in Christ and commitment
to His church. One cannot exist without the other,
as demonstrated in Acts, where no one was counted
as a Christian until he or she was baptized
and received into the community of God's people.*

Robert W. Patterson

I've seen football fans who've painted themselves purple to match the color of their team, shaved the name of their team into their haircuts, worn silly rubber mascot masks, tattooed the team logo onto their shoulders, and even shortened their honeymoons, all in the name of loyalty. However, if for no other reason than sheer longevity, none of these expressions of *fan*atic enthusiasm can compare with the support of Giles Pellerin for the University of Southern California Trojan football team.

Pellerin, eighty-seven years old at this writing, recently attended his seven hundred fiftieth consecutive USC football game. He has not missed a Trojan game—home or away—in sixty-nine years. One year he had an emergency appendectomy just five days before a game. Still hospitalized on Saturday, he told the nurses he was going for a walk and instead went to the stadium.

Why make such sacrifices to identify with an athletic team? Pellerin's answer: "But that's just all part of being a fan."[1]

Though few go to Pellerin's extremes, there are millions

throughout the world whose actions prove that they agree that "part of being a fan" is to openly demonstrate your dedication. But if you ask many Christians to publicly identify themselves with the Son of God in an unusual way which He Himself specified, they will think it strange, cultlike, or only for the Giles Pellerins of the religious world. Some feel self-conscious about such public displays of devotion.

That's the response of many to the idea of Christian baptism. Even some who truly love Christ consider baptism insignificant or something to think about "tomorrow." How important is it? Why should anyone seek baptism in a local church?

BAPTISM OPENLY IDENTIFIES YOU AS A FOLLOWER OF CHRIST

"The Lord knew that the Pharisees had heard that Jesus made and baptized more disciples than John [the Baptist]," records the apostle John (4:1), although Jesus didn't do the actual baptizing (His disciples did). Thousands often flocked to Jesus—some to be healed, some to see a miracle, many just to gawk at this far-famed Galilean man. But others went further by committing themselves to be Christ's disciples and submitting to a baptism that publicly marked them as His.

The last words of Jesus before He ascended into Heaven, according to Matthew 28:19, were "Go therefore and make disciples of all the nations, baptizing them in the name of the Father and of the Son and of the Holy Spirit." The timing of this command of Christ is significant. He has now completed His work of living, dying, and rising from the dead in order to "purify for Himself His own special people" (Titus 2:14). Before He returns to heaven, He gives what has been called the "Great Commission" about making "disciples of all the nations."

Notice that the first thing Jesus said about those who become His disciples is that He wants them to be baptized. Baptism is the Christ-ordained way of openly identifying yourself as a follower of Jesus Christ.

Experiencing baptism doesn't make you right with God. The water of baptism does not wash away the guilt of your disobedience to the laws of God. Rather it is the grace of God, through the work of Jesus Christ, that brings you into God's family and favor. That doesn't mean, however, that baptism is unimportant. Although baptism is never *equated* with faith or salvation in the New Testament, it is closely *associated* with both.

For example, when Peter preached on the Day of Pentecost, that day when the Holy Spirit first came upon all who were followers of Jesus, Acts 2:41 reports this response by some of Peter's listeners: "Then those who gladly received his word were baptized; and that day about three thousand souls were added to them."

When Saul of Tarsus, who later became known as the apostle Paul, became a believer in Jesus Christ, "he arose and was baptized" (Acts 9:18). Later when Paul was in the Grecian city of Philippi, a jailer implored him, "What must I do to be saved?" The answer was, "Believe on the Lord Jesus Christ, and you will be saved, you and your household" (Acts 16:30–31). "And immediately," says verse 33, "he and all his family were baptized."

Baptism was—and should be—the first public expression of faith by those who confess Jesus Christ as Lord and Savior. "Baptism," says England's Erroll Hulse, "is a testimony to the world. Their gaze is not to be discouraged. Our Lord was baptized in public. The baptisms at Pentecost were not secret. . . . Baptism is a testimony to a new life."[2]

When Caffy took vows of marriage to me that cold Saturday night in January, she accepted a ring from me and changed her last name to mine. Because of her love, she was not ashamed to outwardly identify herself with me. Christians are part of the church, which is compared in Ephesians 5:31–32 to a bride for Christ. Those who confess their love for Christ may call themselves by His name—*Christ*ian. To receive baptism in His name is like receiving a wedding ring. It marks you as one who belongs to Christ.

If you love Christ and are part of His bride, why wouldn't you identify yourself with Him in the way He asks? Why would you be ashamed or unwilling to express your love to Him before others in this way? If you are a disciple of Jesus Christ but have never been baptized in His name, now is the time to present yourself to your local church for baptism and show in this uniquely Christian way that you are His.

BAPTISM OPENLY OBEYS THE COMMAND OF CHRIST

Some may wonder, *Isn't baptism just a formality started by men centuries ago? Why can't we rethink it in light of our own culture?*

Baptism is no mere custom started by ancient church leaders, then passed down from generation to generation as an encrusted ecclesiastical tradition or meaningless religious ritual. Baptism is a practice ordained by Jesus Christ Himself.

Let's look again at Jesus' Great Commission to the church: "Go therefore and make disciples of all the nations, baptizing them in the name of the Father and of the Son and of the Holy Spirit, teaching them to observe all things that I have commanded you; and lo, I am with you always, even to the end of the age" (Matthew 28:19–20). Both the original language of this verse and our modern translation agree—Jesus commanded baptism for those who become His disciples.

I find two things especially interesting about the context of this command. First, look at the words of Jesus in the preceding verse: "All authority has been given to Me in heaven and on earth. Go *therefore* and make disciples of all the nations, baptizing them . . ." (italics added). Jesus bases His bidding that we be baptized on His complete authority over all creation. He is not pleading as a religious recruiter anxiously hoping that some of us will be persuaded to join His cause. Christ does not stand here as a great teacher instructing us with mystical insight about something He calls baptism. He isn't acting as a spiritually wise man appealing to us with the advantages of baptism.

Jesus expressly connects His directive about baptism to His authority as God and Lord over all. Even if there were no other reasons, we should be baptized because the King of the universe, the One who made us and owns us and the One who will judge us, has commanded it.

Next, notice what is on the other end of Jesus' baptismal imperative: "I am with you always, even to the end of the age." This reminds us that the King's command remains in force to the end of the world. As long as people become disciples of Jesus, it is His will that the church baptize them. He did not make baptism optional for different cultures, times, personalities, or preferences.

So then, for a disciple of Christ to know His will about baptism and then willingly refuse it is to intentionally disobey Christ and sin against God.

BAPTISM OPENLY EXPRESSES
YOUR FAITH IN MANY TRUTHS

Christian baptism is symbolic of many things. To submit to baptism says that you believe what baptism represents.

God Is Triune

Jesus instructed His disciples to be baptized "in the name of the Father and of the Son and of the Holy Spirit" (Matthew 28:19). This is also more of the language of identification. Baptism *"in the name of the Father and of the Son and of the Holy Spirit"* is another way of identifying yourself with each member of the Trinity. In other words, you are not being baptized in the name of Moses, or the name of the apostle Paul, or the name of your church or pastor, but rather in the name of the triune God. Thus you are declaring allegiance and devotion to the God of the Bible. You are saying, "I belong to Him."

By submitting to a baptism where "the name of the Father and of the Son and of the Holy Spirit" is spoken over you, you are agreeing with the teaching that God is Triune. You are saying through your baptism that you believe there is only one God who is three persons. As the old English minister Matthew Henry, perhaps the best-known of all Bible commentators, put it, "We are baptized not into the *names,* but into the *name* of the Father, Son, and Spirit, which plainly intimates that *these Three are One,* and *their name One.*"[3]

By affirming this mysterious but historic and orthodox belief, you deny several heresies, including *tritheism,* that is, that there are three different persons who *together* become God. You also renounce *pluralism,* the heresy that there are three gods. You further reject *unitarianism,* a belief that affirms there is one God, but which denies the divinity of Jesus Christ and of the Holy Spirit. Additionally, you spurn *modalism,* which teaches that the Father, Son, and Holy Spirit were never God simultaneously. Even if you haven't heard of these dangerous theological errors, when you are baptized "in the name of the Father and of the Son and of the Holy Spirit" you align yourself with the truth of the Trinity of God.

Baptism "in the name of the Father and of the Son and of the Holy Spirit" confesses your belief that each member of the Trinity is involved in your salvation and that you are brought into a relationship with each. God the Father chose you before the foundation of the world (Ephesians 1:3–6). God the Son died a bloody, painful death to make you right with the Father (Romans 5:1, 9–10; Galatians 2:16). God the Holy Spirit opened your eyes, enabling you to see your need to be reconciled to God and to believe in the work of Jesus Christ (John 16:8; 1 Corinthians 2:12; Titus 3:5; 1 Peter 1:2). New Testament baptism affirms that God does His saving work as Father, Son, and Spirit.

An old hymn declares rightly, "Jesus Saves." And some religious groups in America will emphatically tell you they baptize in the name of "Jesus only." But Jesus does not save apart from the Father and the Holy Spirit. Christian baptism was designed by Jesus to acknowledge the role of each person in the triune Godhead in your salvation.

Your Sins Have Been Washed Away

Water baptism doesn't wash away sins; rather, it symbolizes cleansing. The baptismal water which washes the body pictures the cleansing of the soul. The outward act of baptism portrays the inward purification that comes through faith in Jesus Christ. So those who believe their sins have been washed away by Christ should experience the ordinance of Christ that illustrates it.

In the course of his famous sermon to the thousands gathered in Jerusalem in Acts 2, Peter proclaimed, "Repent, and let every one of you be baptized in the name of Jesus Christ for the remission of sins; and you shall receive the gift of the Holy Spirit" (v. 38).

Some have taken the words "be baptized in the name of Jesus Christ *for* the remission of sins" to mean that the forgiveness (remission) of sins and reception of "the gift of the Holy Spirit" occur at the time of baptism. This is incorrect. When you see a poster that says: "WANTED: John Doe *for* Murder," that doesn't mean John Doe is wanted *for the purpose of* murdering someone, but he is wanted because he *already has* murdered someone. Likewise, the Bible teaches here that those who have repented of their sin and believed in Jesus Christ for the remission of sins should be baptized *because* their sins are now forgiven. It affirms that repenting believers are given the gift of the Holy Spirit when they repent and believe. Do you believe God has forgiven your sins? If so, have you been baptized?

Sometimes those who believe in baptismal regeneration (the view that a person is regenerated—born again—at the time of water baptism) also point to Acts 22:16. In this passage the apostle Paul is telling the story of his conversion from Judaism to faith in Christ. After Jesus appeared to him in a blinding vision on the road to Damascus, Paul, then known as Saul of Tarsus, was unable to see for three days. A believer in Damascus was sent by the Lord to deliver a message to Saul. The conclusion of that message was this: "And now why are you waiting? Arise and be baptized, and wash away your sins, calling on the name of the Lord."

Did Saul wash away his sins by receiving baptism? No, the grammar of the original language of this verse makes clear that it is the work of the Lord (not our work) that washes away sins. And it's the "calling on the name of the Lord," not baptism, that is instrumental in forgiveness. A person may be baptized every day, but unless he genuinely calls on the name of the Lord there is absolutely no benefit in the baptism.

Furthermore, it is not "calling on the name of the Lord" *plus* baptism that results in the washing away of sins. To do this would be adding our work to the work of Christ, who lived and died and rose again for our salvation. It would mean that Jesus is not sufficient as a Savior. Our salvation would also be dependent upon our own baptismal actions as well as the efforts of another to baptize us. A right relationship with God would no longer be totally by the grace of God. Part of the glory of our salvation would then belong to us because we participated in the righteous act of baptism.

But Paul contends in Titus 3:5, "Not by works of righteousness which we have done, but according to His mercy He saved us, through the washing of regeneration and renewing of the Holy Spirit." God saves us, and He does so "through the washing of regeneration and renewing of the Holy Spirit," not the washing of baptism. Notice that baptism is not mentioned at all in this passage. Although baptism is an important practice, if it were essential for salvation, we would always see it mentioned when the Bible talks about being made right with God. But as a reading of the New Testament passages on salvation will reveal, baptism is strikingly absent from many of these sections.

You Have Been United with Christ in His Death and Resurrection

Your submission to baptism also announces your faith in the Bible's teaching about the believer's identification with Christ. Read what the apostle Paul says about this great doctrine in Romans 6:3–5: "Or do you not know that as many of us as were baptized into Christ Jesus were baptized into His death? Therefore we were buried with Him through baptism into death, that just as Christ was raised from the dead by the glory of the Father, even so we also should walk in newness of life. For if we have been united together in the likeness of His death, certainly we also shall be in the likeness of His resurrection."

It's important to understand that the baptism spoken of here is not primarily water baptism but a spiritual baptism. When we are born again, the Holy Spirit baptizes, or places us, "into" Jesus Christ. Paul spoke similarly elsewhere when he said, "For by one Spirit we were all baptized into one body—whether Jews or Greeks, whether slaves or free—and have all been made to drink into one Spirit" (1 Corinthians 12:13). So the Holy Spirit puts, or baptizes, us "into Christ Jesus" and "into one body," i.e., the body of Christ.

Obviously these passages do not teach that we are *physically* placed into the *human* body of Jesus Christ. So this baptism is something done in the *spiritual* realm. There is a mysterious, but true, spiritual unity that the Creator has created between Christ and those who believe in Him.

Notice that in Romans 6:3–5, God accounts our unity with Christ from the time of His death and resurrection and credits us with their benefits. God considers what happened to Jesus to have happened to you. You have received the punishment for your sins (by virtue of being united with Christ who received punishment) and have risen from the dead (in Christ), never to be subject to the penalty of sin again.

When you marry, you assume mutual ownership of both the debts and the wealth of your spouse. Even though you did nothing to gather either, they become yours. Similarly, when you are married to, that is, united with, Christ by faith, you share in the accrual of His work. In His love, He assumes the debt of all your sin against God and pays what is due. But He also allows you to share in His wealth—acceptance by God and eternal life. The value and accomplishments of what Jesus did two thousand years ago became yours now and forever when the Spirit of God wed you to Christ.

Now here's the point: Water baptism symbolizes this unity. It is a statement of faith that you have been placed into Christ, bonded with Him spiritually. Receiving baptism with water expresses your belief that you have received the baptism by the Spirit into Christ. Why would anyone who has known the immeasurable blessing of eternal union with Jesus Christ not want to receive the sign of it?

Through Christ God Has Given You a New Life

Baptism announces to the world that you have a new life in Christ. You emerge from the baptismal experience a living testimony to the truth of 2 Corinthians 5:17: "Therefore, if anyone is in Christ, he is a new creation; old things have passed away; behold, all things have become new."

"I've been changed," your baptism exclaims: "I'm not the person I was before meeting Christ. I'm alive to God now. My life is different—my thoughts, my actions, my heart, my perspective—they're all new."

This symbolic connection between baptism and a new life is suggested in Romans 6:4: "Therefore we were buried with Him through baptism into death, that just as Christ was raised from the dead by the glory of the Father, even so we also should walk in *newness of life*" (italics added). As noted earlier, this text speaks of spiritual baptism, i.e., being united with Christ, a reality symbolized by water baptism.

Jesus avowed, "I am the resurrection and the life" (John 11:25), and proved it by His resurrection to new life. Those who have been united with the living Christ, the God-man who "was raised from the dead by the glory of the Father," are united with *life*. This new life—*eternal* life—transforms them from the inside out. Planted and growing within them are new loves (love for God, love for His Word, love for His people), new desires (for purity, for holy living, for heaven), new priorities (the will of God), and more. This is not merely turning over a new leaf, but being given a new *life*. Baptism is both a testimony to this new life within and a pledge to "walk in newness of life."

PRACTICAL PRINCIPLES REGARDING BAPTISM

Baptism is not a saving ritual.

Although this has been said already, it cannot be overemphasized. The error of salvation through baptism is universally one of the most common misconceptions of Christianity. You could be baptized once an hour for the rest of your life and never be right with God.

Even though baptism is an act of obedience to Jesus, it is *not* a *saving* act. The only saving act in history is the death and resurrection of Jesus Christ. Our responsibility is to believe in *that* work, not to try to augment it by baptism.

Baptism can strengthen your assurance of salvation.

In 1 Peter 3:21 baptism is connected to "the answer of a good conscience toward God." If you neglect baptism, you can expect consequences in your conscience. This single act of disobedience could mean the difference between having and not having the assurance that you are right with God.

Several times in my pastoral experience I baptized people—young and old—who procrastinated about it. After they became Christians and were taught about baptism, they hesitated. The longer they delayed, the more uncertain they became of their relationship with Christ. Following baptism, however, their drooping spiritual life flourished like a wilted plant newly watered. I recall one case where not only family members but also unbelieving friends remarked about the change in the woman's life following her belated baptism. The roots of her relationship with Christ deepened and she became much more fruitful.

Do you struggle with assurance of salvation? If you claim to follow Christ but you have never followed His command to be baptized, your doubts are yet another signal of what you need to do.

Baptism is for you if you know Christ.

If you have had the experience symbolized by baptism, but have never been baptized, present yourself to your church as a candidate for baptism.

It's easy to understand why someone who has never been united with Christ would have no desire for baptism. But why would anyone who has come to know Jesus Christ and received His eternal life refuse to identify with Him in the manner He prescribed? If others (perhaps even you) will proudly wear clothing announcing their loyalty to a sports team, if Giles Pellerin will travel the country for sixty-nine years to express his devotion to the USC football team, can you remain unwilling to identify yourself with your Savior and God through baptism?

Perhaps you still have some unanswered questions. Talk with your pastor about them. Don't put it off any longer. Do the will of Christ and be baptized.

As Saul of Tarsus was asked in Acts 22:16, "And now why are you waiting? Arise and be baptized."

CHAPTER THREE

WHY JOIN A CHURCH?

. . . . ✤ . . . .

Scripture makes abundantly clear that we
are to be members of a local church.
Kenneth Kantzer

Why should I join the church?"

Despite my seminary training and pastoral experience, I was unprepared for this new Christian's question. He agreed from our study of the Scripture that he needed to identify himself as a disciple of Christ through baptism, but he asked, "Can you show me from the New Testament that I'm supposed to *officially join* anything?"

Now he really had me.

"If I come and worship as often as the members," he continued, "if I fellowship with these believers as much as anyone else, if I profit from the teaching and other ministries of the church, and if I actively demonstrate love for my brothers and sisters in Christ here, why should I formally join the church?"

His question struck me with an uncomfortable logic.

I began to realize that many of my conclusions about church membership were actually nothing more than previously unchallenged assumptions. These assumptions were now melting into questions of my own. Can I give reasons from Scripture why anyone should join a church? Did the Christians in New Testament times formally join churches, or did they have more of an informal relationship? Did the churches in the days of the apostle Paul have a membership list? How do I respond to the rising tide of opinion that says church membership is merely an unchallenged, but unbiblical, tradition and an unnecessary formality?

Here's what I found.

SCRIPTURE INDICATES CHURCH MEMBERSHIP IN NEW TESTAMENT TIMES

We encounter the word *church* throughout the New Testament. In the great majority of instances the term refers to a specific *local church* like that in Rome or Corinth. Sometimes when we read of the church, the reference is to what's often called the "church universal," that is, all Christians everywhere. But "church" in the Bible almost always means "local church."

At the very least, the local church was the fellowship of the followers of Jesus Christ in a particular area. We know that they met together, worshiped together, prayed together, and so forth as the born-again family of God. But did people actually join this fellowship in some official way, or was it a mutually assumed and less formal association? Several things from the New Testament make sense only in the context of an official membership.

The Instructions for Church Discipline

In Matthew 18:15–17, Jesus gave us instructions on how the church should respond when someone within the church persists in living like an unbeliever. We read of a specific case of this in 1 Corinthians 5 when the apostle Paul, writing under the inspiration of the Holy Spirit, instructed the Christians in the church at Corinth to handle it. In verses 11–13 Paul says,

> But now I have written to you not to keep company with anyone named a brother, who is sexually immoral, or covetous, or an idolater, or a reviler, or a drunkard, or an extortioner—not even to eat with such a person. For what have I to do with judging those also who are outside? Do you not judge those who are inside? But those who are outside God judges. Therefore "put away from yourselves the evil person."

There was a sexually immoral man in this church. Was Paul simply telling them not to let this man come to church with them because he was acting like an unbeliever instead of a Christian? No, he couldn't have meant that, for we know from other places in this letter (cf. 14:24–25) that unbelievers were welcome to attend church meetings.

Even when they obeyed Paul's instructions to "put away from your-selves the evil person" and consider the man an unbeliever, they would have allowed (even welcomed) him to come and sit under the preaching of God's Word like any other person in town. So in what sense would they have "put away" ("remove"—NASB, "expel"—NIV) this man?

The best way of explaining how they would have put away this man is to understand that they removed him from the membership of the church and generally stopped associating with him outside the church meetings.

Notice that Paul refers to those who are "inside" and to those who are "outside." Outside of what? As we've noted, anyone could attend their meetings. This kind of language can only refer to a defi-nite church membership of converted people. For what authority does a group have to remove someone who is already "outside" and not a member of the group?

You can't fire someone who doesn't work for you. You can't vote to remove a government official elected by another country. You can't appeal to a court to discipline someone who isn't within its juris-diction. In the same way, you can't formally discipline someone who is in an informal relationship with you; you have no authority to do so. These people in Corinth had voluntarily committed themselves to a formal relationship, and they knew who were official members of the church and who were "outside."

Church discipline must be done by the "church" (Matthew 18:17) and occur "when you are gathered together" (1 Corinthians 5:4). Who is to gather together? How do you know who the church is? How do you determine who does or does not have the right to speak and vote on such matters?

Does the person subject to discipline have the liberty to bring in his extended family or co-workers who have never been to the church, or even people off the street, and expect them to be given an equal say with those who have been faithful to the church for years? Why not? Do you exclude them from involvement because they've never been part of the church? Then what about the person who attended once five years ago? Or those who came at Easter and Christmas last year? Or those who regularly watch the church services on television or listen to them on the radio, and perhaps even send money, but never enter the building? Or those from distant cities who visit several times each year because of family members in the church? Obviously, biblical church discipline must be limited to a specific group—and that must mean the church *members*.

The Meaning of the Word "Join"

In Acts 5:13 we read of the reaction of the non-Christians in Jerusalem after a couple within the church, Ananias and Sapphira, had died on the spot when it was revealed that they had lied to the church. It says, "Yet none of the rest dared join them, but the people esteemed them highly." The unbelievers had great respect for the Christians, but for a while after this incident none who claimed to be believers but were merely superficial believers wanted to join the church.

In the Greek language in which Paul wrote this letter, the word he used that's translated here as *join* literally means "to glue or cement together, to unite, to join firmly." It doesn't refer to an informal, merely assumed sort of relationship, but one where you choose to "glue" or "join" yourself firmly to the others. Again, that kind of language only makes sense in the context of membership.

That same "glue word" is used in the New Testament to describe being joined together in a sexual relationship (1 Corinthians 6:16) and being joined to the Lord in one spirit in salvation (1 Corinthians 6:17). And it's the same word Paul uses in 1 Corinthians 5:11 when he says "not to keep company with anyone named a brother" who continues in immorality, but rather "to put away from yourselves the evil person." Clearly this kind of language doesn't refer to a casual, superficial, or informal relationship.

So when it says in Acts 5:13 that no insincere believer dared join them for a while, the glue word used there speaks of such a cohesive, bonding relationship that it must be referring to a recognized church membership.

The Meaning of "the Whole Church"

The earthly founder of the church at Corinth, the apostle Paul, wrote to this new body of Christians about their many difficulties, including how to bring order to their public worship. He began 1 Corinthians 14:23 with, "Therefore if the whole church comes together in one place . . ." Who did he have in mind when he referred to "the whole church"? The only realistic answer is the church members. That's why one commentator, working with the original language of this text, translates it "If then the whole church assembles together and all *its members*" [italics added] and notes "(the last two words are not in the Greek but are naturally to be understood)."[1]

Imagine the leaders of the Corinthian Christians walking into the gathering of the church for worship one Sunday. Would they have known by looking, or would they have had some way of deciding whether "the whole church" was there? Surely they would have known who was supposed to be present in a churchwide meeting and who was missing. But how else could they have known when "the whole church" was "together in one place" without knowing who was a member and who wasn't? This implies a verifiable membership.

The Instructions for Pastoral Oversight and Spiritual Leadership

"This is a faithful saying," said Paul to Timothy. "If a man desires the position of a bishop, he desires a good work" (1 Timothy 3:1). In other places the New Testament also refers to a bishop, or "overseer" as the NIV and NASB render it, as a pastor, shepherd, or elder (Acts 20:17, 28; Philippians 1:1; Titus 1:5–7). But what or whom does he oversee? How can he provide spiritual oversight if he doesn't know exactly those for whom he is responsible? A distinguishable, mutually understood membership is required for him to fulfill his charge.

First Timothy 3:5 says of an overseer, "For if a man does not know how to rule his own house, how will he take care of the church of God?" The local church is compared to a family. Is anyone a casual member of a family? No, membership in a family is a very definite thing.

"Take heed to yourselves," Paul instructed the elders of the church of Ephesus, "and to all the flock" (Acts 20:28). How could they fulfill their responsibility as undershepherds to "all the flock" unless they knew who was part of the flock and who was not? These leaders of a growing church in a large city needed some means of identification of those for whom they were to take heed. A simple membership list is the logical solution.

In Hebrews 13:17 is a word addressed to those under such overseers: "Obey those who rule over you, and be submissive, for they watch out for your souls, as those who must give account. Let them do so with joy and not with grief, for that would be unprofitable for you." For whom will the leaders of a church give an account—everyone who comes in and out of their church services? No, it has to be a limited group of people—the members of the church—for whom they will be answerable. How can church leaders be responsible for someone until they know he or she is committed to their care? The Bible's instructions for pastoral oversight and spiritual leadership can best be obeyed when there is a well-defined church membership.

The Biblical Metaphors Used to Describe Local Churches

The New Testament uses several metaphors to describe churches. Some of these metaphors describe the church of Christ collectively throughout the world. Although all of them could potentially apply to the local church also, at least four of these metaphors—flock, temple, body, and household—are definitely used to refer to individual churches (in Acts 20:28; Ephesians 2:21; 1 Corinthians 12:27; and 1 Timothy 3:15). And each metaphor is best understood in a setting of specific church membership.

A *flock* of sheep isn't a random collection of ewes, rams, and lambs. Shepherds know their flocks. They know which sheep are theirs to care for and which are not. Sheep belong to specific flocks. This is also the way it should be for God's spiritual sheep. A *temple* building, just like a church building, shouldn't have any loose bricks or blocks. If it does, something's wrong. Each one of them has a definite place. "There is no place," said an English preacher long ago, "for any loose stone in God's edifice."[2]

The same analogy is true for a human *body.* Your body isn't a casual collection of loosely related parts. You don't keep your fingers in your pocket until you need them. They are joined. They are members of the body. The local body of Christ should be like this also—those joined to Christ, who are members of His body, should express that relationship through a visible membership. And in a *household,* a family, you're either a member or you're not. So if you are part of the family of God, show it by joining a local expression of God's family.

British pastor Eric Lane sees additional significance in this quartet of metaphors:

God has given us four pictures of the church, not one. This is not just to emphasize and prove the point by repetition, but also to say four different things about what it means to be a member of a church. To be a stone in his temple means to belong to a worshipping community. To be part of a body means to belong to a living, functioning, serving, witnessing community. To be a sheep in the flock means belonging to a community dependent on him for food, protection, and direction. To be a member of a family is to belong to a community bound by a common father-hood. Put together you have the main functions of an individual Christian. Evidently we are meant to fulfill these not on our own but together in the church. Now can you see the answer to the question why you should join a church?[3]

We've just seen five biblical indications that New Testament churches had membership lists of some sort. They knew who was a member and who was not. When people became followers of Jesus, or when followers of Jesus moved to another town, they formally identified themselves with a local church—they *joined* it. "In the New Testament there is no such person as a Christian who is not a church member," writes Douglas G. Millar. "Conversion was described as 'the Lord adding to the church' (Acts 2:47). There was no spiritual drifting."[4]

Perhaps you are persuaded that the churches in the days of the New Testament had membership lists and that people joined the churches instead of drifting. Are there other biblical reasons why Christians should be members of a church today?

THERE ARE BIBLICAL REASONS FOR JOINING A CHURCH

You Prove That You're Not Ashamed to Identify with Christ or His People

Jesus said (in Mark 8:38) that if anyone is ashamed to identify himself with Him on earth then He will not identify Himself with that person when he or she stands before God in the Judgment. Joining a church is one of the plainest ways of saying you're not ashamed to identify yourself with Jesus and with His people.

Jesus certainly made a formal commitment to identify Himself with His people when He left heaven to come to earth and die as a man. Can, then, one for whom Christ died be reluctant to identify himself formally with the others for whom Christ died? California pastor John MacArthur explains and asks further, "You have been joined together with Christ. . . . You bear His name. Are you ashamed to belong? Are you ashamed to bear that identification with other believers of like precious faith? . . . Shouldn't you be willing outwardly to identify with the visible, gathered members of that group to which you eternally belong?"[5]

When you join a church you make it clear whose side you're on. You're telling the family of God that you're part of the family too, and that you don't want to be considered on the outside (1 Corinthians 5:12–13) any longer.

You Stop Being an Independent Christian

In Matthew 18:15–17, Jesus set up an accountability system. When a professing believer starts living like an unbeliever, those in the church who know about it are to confront him in love about his sin. First, one is to go to this person, and then, if he will not listen, that one is to bring one or two others along for a second conversation. The goal is to restore him to full fellowship with the Lord and his fellow believers. If he persistently and unrepentantly refuses to return to the Lord, the final step is to report the matter to the church. Then everyone in the church has the chance to win the person back. And if he continues in his sin, the church is to withdraw fellowship from him as the final means of showing him his need to repent.

If you aren't part of the church, it has no authority over you and cannot do what Jesus said to do. Unless you join the church, your independence places you outside the way Jesus wants things to happen.

Related to this idea of spiritual authority, recall Hebrews 13:17, the passage that tells us to obey the leaders of the church and submit to them because they keep watch over our souls. The leaders of the church are to watch over you by providing spiritual protection for you and caring about your growth in Christ. You place yourself outside that spiritual watch and care unless you join a local church.

You Participate in a Stronger, More Unified Effort of God's People

I've met a few people who weren't interested in church membership but who were zealously witnessing to others about Christ and trying to make disciples for Him. Since they do so well what relatively few Christians do at all, why emphasize church membership to them? They need to see that joining a church is like putting one candle with many others. They will give off more light collectively than one lone candle ever could, and together they will have a greater penetration into the world's darkness.

And as your local church reaches across the country and around the world in direct and indirect support of missionary work, you can participate in ways of reaching the world for Christ that you could have never dreamed otherwise.

In contrast, consider the potential negative impact on our efforts to talk about Jesus if we don't join His earthly body. How believable is our testimony of the goodness and greatness of Christ if we don't want to identify openly with Christ's family?

You Have a Greater Opportunity to Use Your Spiritual Gift

At the moment of salvation when the Holy Spirit comes to live within a believer in Christ, He brings a gift with Him. "There are diversities of gifts, but the same Spirit," Paul writes in 1 Corinthians 12:4. He continues in verse 11, "But one and the same Spirit works all these things, distributing to each one individually as He wills." For what purpose does God give each Christian a gift? The answer is in verse 7: "But the manifestation of the Spirit is given to each one for the profit of all." God gifts you individually so that you will use your gift "for the profit" of others. You have a greater opportunity to do that when you use your gift in and through local church membership.

Yes, you can use your spiritual gift for the good of God's people without joining a church. But in a lot of churches, many of the ministry opportunities are available for church members only. That's because the church wants to know that you stand with her doctrinally and support her ministry goals before you're asked to minister in certain positions. Besides, remaining outside the membership of the church (unless providentially hindered) may say more about your desire to serve than you intend. "Not joining the church," according to MacArthur, "is saying, 'I don't want to serve the only institution Christ ever built.'"[6] So the best way to maximize the effectiveness of your spiritual gift is to use it "for the profit of all" in a local church as a member.

You Openly Demonstrate the Reality of the Body of Christ

"Now you are the body of Christ," Paul wrote to the church at Corinth, "and each one of you is a part of it" (1 Corinthians 12:27 NIV). But how can the body of Christ be seen? When you join a church, you make it visible. You give a living demonstration of the spiritual reality of the body of Christ. You show that even though you are an individual, you are a part of the body and you are joined together with others. You take the body of Christ out of the realm of the theoretical and give it a meaning that people can see.

As pastor and author Ben Patterson puts it, "To join a particular part of the body of Christ is not to bring something into existence that was not there before. It is simply to make actual what is spiritual, to prove that the spiritual is real."[7]

You Participate in a More Balanced Ministry

In Ephesians 4:11–16 we read of the Lord giving gifted men such as evangelists and pastor-teachers to the church. We're taught that each part—every member—of the church body has a job to do for the body to function properly and grow. It's a picture of wholeness and balance. We need this God-ordained mutual ministry to be what God intends.

Further, God has designed us so that we can't get this well-rounded ministry on our own. No one develops the proper spiritual symmetry just by listening to Christian radio, watching Christian television, or reading Christian books. You can't get this kind of maturity merely by participating in a group Bible study. Unless you're an active part of a local church, your Christian life and ministry will be imbalanced.

You Demonstrate Your Commitment "to the Proper Working of Each Individual Part"

Some time ago, *Moody,* the magazine of Moody Bible Institute in Chicago, made an interesting observation about the hitchhiker. He wants a free ride. He assumes no responsibility for the money needed to buy the car, the gas to run it, or the cost of maintenance. He expects a comfortable ride and adequate safety. He assumes the driver has insurance covering him in case of an accident. He thinks little of asking the driver to take him to a certain place even though it may involve extra miles or inconvenience.

Think about the "spiritual hitchhiker" who has settled all his major questions and has definitely decided where he wants to attend church, but now he wants all the benefits and privileges of that church's ministry without taking any responsibility for it. His attitude is all take and no give. He wants no accountability, just a free ride.

This is not meant to discourage those who are attending a church to find answers about Jesus Christ and are still uncertain about their eternal destiny. If that describes you, your first priority is to come to Christ rather than to come for church membership.

Neither is this intended to deter those who are sincerely and actively seeking God's will in a decision about a church home. Sometimes that decision cannot be made quickly. A wise person evaluates a church carefully before joining its membership.

A spiritual hitchhiker, however, has no real intention of joining the church, at least not soon. He only wants to enjoy its advantages without any obligation on his part. He wants convenience without commitment, to be served rather than to serve. But every true Christian is to be committed to "the proper working of each individual part" (Ephesians 4:16 NASB) in a local church. When you join a church, you're saying you believe in taking *your* individual part and that you don't want to be a spiritual hitchhiker.

You Encourage New Believers to Commitment to the Local Body of Christ

In the familiar passage on church commitment, Hebrews 10:24–25 says, "And let us consider one another in order to stir up love and good works, not forsaking the assembling of ourselves together, as is the manner of some, but exhorting one another, and so much the more as you see the Day approaching."

Notice the command to "consider one another" that is associated here with church involvement. Bear in mind the message you give to other believers, especially new believers, if you do *not* join a church. What are you modeling to new believers when you remain uncommitted to the local church? Do they see your example and learn that the church isn't important enough to join? Do they get the message that the kingdom of God is not worth such an investment of yourself? Do they interpret your actions as saying that the work of God does not deserve a full commitment?

On the other hand, joining a church is one way of "exhorting one another," as this passage puts it, "to love and good works." When you join the local church you provide a positive example that says, "It is worth being a part of this, and I recommend it to you."

You Encourage a Ministry When You Consider It Faithful and Join It

Suppose John loves Mary and sees no one else but her for ten years. Every time they are together he tells her that he loves her, but he never proposes to her. Finally, after a decade she has enough nerve to ask him, "John, why haven't you wanted to marry me?"

If he says, "I'm just trying to make sure," how do you think she will feel? Of course, she's glad he says he loves her, and she's thankful for all he does for her, and she's pleased that he doesn't see anyone else, but in spite of all that, she's going to be somewhat discouraged because he doesn't love her enough to decisively commit himself to her.

The people and pastor of a church are glad whenever you attend. But if you keep coming and never join, they may begin to wonder what Mary wondered about John, despite how happy you seem to be with the church and how many wonderful things you say about it. There is a sense in which your attendance and involvement can actually discourage the church and its leaders if, after a reasonable time, you do not join it.

Conversely, the church is encouraged (the NASB and NIV render "exhort" in Hebrews 10:25 as "encourage"), and its leadership is encouraged, when you indicate by joining the church that you love it and think it is a biblically faithful ministry worthy of your commitment.

BIBLICAL RESPONSES TO THIS MESSAGE

Now that you've read these things about church membership, what should you do?

Turn from living for yourself and follow Christ, the Head of the church.

Membership in a local church does not mean that you are part of the body of Christ. Without Christ, church membership means nothing. Hell is filled with people who were church members. Before you respond to the challenge of church membership, you must make sure you know Jesus Christ, who "is head over all things to the church" (Ephesians 1:22). Your greatest need in life is not to be on the membership roll of a church; it is to be made right with God by the One who died for the church, who created the church, who loves the church, and who is returning someday for His true church.

What should you do? The Bible says you should "repent, and believe in the gospel" (Mark 1:15)—the message about the life, death, and resurrection of Jesus Christ. To repent and believe in this way involves turning from living for yourself and turning, in faith, to Jesus Christ. Recognize that your sin has separated you from God (Isaiah 59:2; Romans 3:23). You've repeatedly broken God's laws, and this excludes you from His family and from eternity with Him. Come to Christ, however, and He can make you right with God. Believe that His death can cleanse you from all guilt before God and provide you with all the righteousness God requires. This is infinitely more important than church membership.

Present yourself to the church for baptism as a symbol of identification with Christ and His church.

Ten days after Jesus had ascended back to heaven, the Holy Spirit of God descended upon the believers who were gathered in Jerusalem. Filled with the Holy Spirit, Peter preached that morning to the crowd that had gathered because of the Jewish Feast of Pentecost. About three thousand people turned from their sin and believed that the crucified and risen Jesus was their Messiah and God. Then, according to Acts 2:41, "those who gladly received his word were baptized." If you have received (believed) the word about Jesus Christ, you should be baptized.

Baptism is a church ordinance commanded by Christ (Matthew 28:19). If you have trusted Jesus Christ as Savior and Lord, you should present yourself to a local church as a candidate for baptism. By this means you will openly identify yourself as a follower of Christ and a member of His body.

Present yourself for membership in a local, New Testament church
if you've been scripturally baptized and your membership is
elsewhere.

Have you come to Christ and been baptized? Then you should formally identify yourself with the people of Christ *where you live*. If you have moved, or for some other reason have membership in a church you no longer attend, you should unite with the believers of a biblically based, Christ-centered church where you can participate faithfully. (See Acts 18:27 and Romans 16:1–2 for a New Testament example of Christians who identified with and served with a local congregation even when they were in a place which might not have been their permanent residence.)

When I was in college I faithfully attended a local church. After about a year I realized that my membership needed to be in that church, not the one back home that I grew up in but now rarely visited. So I presented myself for membership in the church where I was worshiping regularly. Today, I encourage students to become members of a church in their college town, because that's where they are most of the time. This develops a healthy pattern of thinking *Join a church here* whenever they relocate. This habit will serve them well when they graduate and move away from college to who-knows-where.

Reaffirm the commitment implied in your present church membership.

If you are presently a member of the local church you attend, you should exercise your spiritual gifts in and through that church (see Romans 12:5–6a). Membership implies commitment and activity. All the living parts of the body of Christ should be working and fulfilling their God-intended function.

Think about this: a member of a human body, such as a heart or kidney, cannot exist apart from the body, except by some temporary and artificial sustenance. But this isn't what it's designed for. In this sheer existence the organ doesn't fulfill its function in the body. It isn't nourished in the way God intended through the body, but subsists only through some synthetic way that provides mere maintenance but doesn't stimulate growth or development.

In the same way, a true member of Christ's body is *not designed* to operate independently or outside the body. An authentic part of Christ's spiritual body cannot be content while separated from the rest of His earthly body. That's because he or she is made for *inter*dependence, not *in*dependence.

As wonderful and sophisticated as the heart is, it was never made to be just a heart, but a *part* of a *body*. It has no value to the body outside the body. And the heart itself can't thrive outside the body. You were never made just to be an individual Christian, but a *part* of a *body*. As every organ and every cell is God-created to be an active member of the human body, so every true Christian is God-created to be an active member of a local body of Christ.

Are *you* a true Christian? Are you an actively and biblically involved member of a local body of Christ? "Belonging to the church," says John MacArthur, "is at the very heart of Christianity."[8]

Church membership involves many responsibilities, but we must never lose sight of the great privilege that it really is. "We must grasp once again," said Martyn Lloyd-Jones of London in the mid-twentieth century, "the idea of church membership as being the membership of the body of Christ and as the biggest honour which can come a man's way in this world."[9]

CHAPTER FOUR

WHY LISTEN TO PREACHING IN THE CHURCH?

· · · · · · · ❖ · · · · · · ·

The church has to rediscover who God is,
come to know Him, and fellowship with Him.
The avenue for that has always been Bible
exposition and teaching. There's no shortcut.

James Montgomery Boice

Some time ago I received a denominational publication mailed monthly to tens of thousands of churches. It told of a church in a southern state that believed in "staging drama productions *in place of sermons*" (italics added). The associate pastor in charge of this said that drama "is the most effective method of presenting the gospel to the people of today because they are so in tune to the visual." Regarding preaching he said, "We've just got to find other ways to get them in." He made these comments at the first-ever National Drama, Puppetry and Clowning Festival sponsored by this major denomination.

In some quarters of the church today, preaching is seen as the pony express method of delivering the message of the gospel in a day of communication by fax/modem and satellite. Like that horseback postal system, preaching served its purpose in its day, but now there are more effective, efficient, and attractive methods of communicating.

There's no denying this is a visually oriented age. And the day of the sermon being the best and only "show" given by the best-educated man in town did go out in most places with the pony express in the mid-1800s.

Why shouldn't we give preaching a decent burial and eliminate it from our services, or at least minimize it? Why *don't* we replace it with drama? Why not downplay it behind ceremony and ritual as many churches do? Why not show Christian films instead of preaching, or show popular movies and make comments about them or relate the Bible to them? Why not take the time formerly spent on preaching and devote it to more professional and entertaining music, exciting testimonies, or at least a pastor/congregation dialogue? Wouldn't any of those be more appealing in a visually oriented, participative culture than preaching?

In defiance of the world's wisdom that says no one wants to come to church and hear sermons, in defiance of the church marketing strategy that questions the value of traditional preaching and would rather replace it with something more visually stimulating, I want to contend from 1 Corinthians 1:21 that *preaching is always relevant.* Although I could list many reasons from throughout the Bible, here are several from this one verse that show why you should attend a church where you can consistently hear biblical preaching.

GOD WAS PLEASED TO ORDAIN PREACHING

From the ever-contemporary, God-inspired Bible we read, "For since, in the wisdom of God, the world through wisdom did not know God, it pleased God through the foolishness of the message preached to save those who believe" (1 Corinthians 1:21).

When God determined that the world through its wisdom would not be able to know Him, He decreed that we would come to know Him only through a revelation of Himself. He revealed Himself generally through creation (Romans 1:20), but most clearly through a Word. He sent His Son to add humanity to His divinity and become the revelation of God on Earth.

Because He is the perfect declaration of God (John 1:18), Jesus Christ is called "the Word" of God. The apostle John describes the incarnational self-disclosure of God this way: "And the Word became flesh and dwelt among us" (John 1:14). To see God, look at the Word of God, Jesus Christ.

God also revealed Himself through His *written* Word, known to us as the Bible. Near the end of his life, when the apostle Paul wrote his last known letter, he affirmed that "all Scripture is given by inspiration of God, and is profitable for doctrine, for reproof, for correction, for instruction in righteousness" (2 Timothy 3:16). Thus the words of Scripture are the words of God Himself. As such, they are never outdated or stale. On the contrary, "the word of God is living and powerful" (Hebrews 4:12).

Today it is through God's written Word that we come to know His Incarnate Word, Jesus. In other words, God revealed Himself to us in Jesus, and through the Bible we learn about Jesus.

There's much more I could say about God's self-revelation in Scripture, how it reveals His attributes, His laws, His will, His plan for the world. My purpose at this point, however, is to emphasize how God means to make His inspired words and His Son known to the world. The mere presence of the Bible on the planet does not communicate its message. God also has a plan of proclamation.

Think about some of the options available to an omnipotent God for declaring His message. He has tens of thousands of angels. They could be employed full-time throughout the earth declaring the words of God and the story of Jesus, much as they did to the shepherds near Bethlehem the night Jesus was born (Luke 2:9–14).

God created and controls the stars; He could make a galactic Bible of them and communicate to us nightly. God could write with the calligraphy of the clouds in the tongue of every people-group to reveal Himself each day. He could speak every morning directly from heaven in a voice that thunders from the sky, as He did in John 12:28–30.

But for reasons known only to Himself, He has chosen none of these means. Instead He has determined that He would reveal Himself to people through His Word by means of *preaching*. Therefore preaching is always relevant, no matter what a majority of people thinks in any particular culture at a given point in history, because it is God's idea.

The Meaning of Preaching

What does God mean by "preaching"? In a broad sense preaching is proclamation, the proclamation of God's truth by any and every legitimate means. Thus sharing the gospel in a personal conversation is preaching, giving someone an evangelistic book is preaching, teaching a Sunday school lesson about Jesus is preaching, sharing your testimony of conversion to Christ is preaching, writing it in a letter is preaching.

But the word translated "preached" in this verse (1 Corinthians 1:21) implies more than just proclamation, because there is another Greek word that is used for the idea of proclaiming or announcing the Good News about Jesus. If Paul meant to describe the generic proclamation of God's Word in all forms, then he could have chosen that other word. But all major English translations (KJV, NKJV, NIV, NASB, RSV) render this as "preached." When the New Testament wants to refer to what we normally think of as pulpit preaching, this is the word it uses. Pulpit preaching is my emphasis in this chapter.

When Paul says "it pleased God through the foolishness of the message preached to save those who believe," the grammatical emphasis of the words is on the "message" that was preached—the content—not the act of preaching itself. God saves people through His message, the message about Jesus Christ, not through the physical actions of someone preaching. Yet no one is saved unless the message is delivered. And the primary delivery system in the New Testament is what we think of as public preaching.

So while we usually see the New Testament word *preaching* and rightly emphasize that it can refer to anyone's proclamation or distribution, public or private, of the message about Jesus, we have done such a good job of making this clear that we're now in danger of thinking of pulpit preaching as irrelevant and unnecessary. Yet preaching is always relevant because God was pleased to ordain it.

So as I talk about preaching, I am referring to a man of God publicly teaching God's Word with exhortation and application.

The Ordination of Preaching

God ordained preaching in the Old Testament. He could have dropped down some sort of visual images like photographs or paintings describing what He wanted people to know. He could have created a completed book of His words to us and delivered it by angelic express. Instead He spoke through the preaching of prophets.

In the New Testament, Jesus preached. After His thirty years of hiddenness and preparation in Nazareth, and after His forty days of fasting and temptation in the wilderness, when He emerged to begin His ministry, Matthew 4:17 says, "From that time Jesus began to *preach* and to say, 'Repent, for the kingdom of heaven is at hand.'" In Luke 4:43–44 Jesus said, "'I must *preach* the kingdom of God to the other cities also, because for this purpose I have been sent.' And He was *preaching* in the synagogues of Galilee" (italics added).

Then Jesus sent out the apostles to preach. In Matthew 10:7 Jesus commissioned the twelve and said, "And as you go, *preach,* saying, "The kingdom of heaven is at hand.'" Later on, after Jesus' resurrection and ascension, Peter would report of Jesus in Acts 10:42, "And He commanded us to *preach* to the people" (italics added).

Preaching was the method of the apostle Paul. After he was converted, at first no one could believe it. But the word that kept circulating about him, according to Galatians 1:23, was this: "But they were hearing only, 'He who formerly persecuted us now *preaches* the faith which he once tried to destroy'" (italics added).

When Paul described God's call and purpose for his life in 1 Timothy 2:7, he said it was this "for which I was appointed a *preacher* and an apostle—I am speaking the truth in Christ and not lying." That's why Paul said in 1 Corinthians 1:17, "For Christ did not send me to baptize, but to *preach* the gospel" (italics added). That doesn't mean he thought baptism was unimportant; we know from other things he wrote about baptism how he valued it. But he meant that God doesn't save people through baptism, but rather through the gospel. So he wasn't sent just to go around baptizing people, but to *preach.*

Suppose for a moment that you were the apostle. God sends you to one of the major cities of the world, Corinth. You are the only Christian in the entire metropolis and your job is to plant a church. What method would you choose?

Paul could have chosen to get the town's interest through drama. After all, drama started in Greece, and the Corinthian theater of Paul's day is still there. He could have thought, *These Greeks know nothing of the Scriptures, so perhaps I should start by having them acted out so they can better understand what I want to talk about.* But he didn't. He could have reasoned, *They like music,* and come to town with a concert in the theater and built upon that. He might have used a similar approach featuring an Olympic athlete. But what did he do? Basically he just preached (Acts 18:4, 11). Not that the other things might not have had their place, but preaching was (and is) the method explicitly appointed by God.

God's ordained method, preaching, is always relevant because it is timeless, transcultural, and simple. It doesn't require equipment, money, organizations, or buildings. I have preached in enormous edifices with elaborate audio and video equipment, orchestras, and stunning stained-glass windows, but also with the blessing of God in a tiny, half-finished, mud-and-sticks church/hut in the bush country of Kenya.

I have preached mostly in the familiar surroundings of my own culture, but occasionally, and with some apparent fruitfulness, through interpreters in a variety of the world's cultures. I have preached in showplace homes; one-room, dirt-floor hovels; and in the open air. Preaching can occur where there is no electricity, no literature, no literacy. Preaching can adapt to either a high-tech or low-tech society and to everything in between. All that's needed for preaching in any place, in any culture, at any time, is a preacher, the Word of God, and listeners.

Regardless of how inefficient some may think preaching is in our technological, mass media society, regardless of how much more exciting or entertaining or even successful other methods may appear, the most effective way of communicating the gospel of Jesus Christ is still through the means God was pleased to choose—preaching.

"God uses preaching to communicate more than current communication theory is concerned with," writes J. I. Packer; "I have nothing against books, films, tapes, and study groups in their place, but the place where God sets the preacher is not their place."[1]

GOD'S MESSAGE IS THE SUBJECT OF PREACHING

Let me remind you of 1 Corinthians 1:21: "For since, in the wisdom of God, the world through wisdom did not know God, it pleased God through the foolishness of *the message* preached to save those who believe" (italics added).

The content of true biblical preaching is the message of God. Paul explains in verses on either side of verse 21 what he means by the message. In verse 18 he describes it as "the message of the cross." In verses 22–23 he says, "For Jews request a sign, and Greeks seek after wisdom; *but we preach Christ crucified,* to the Jews a stumbling block and to the Greeks foolishness" (italics added).

The centerpiece of the message preached by the church should be Jesus Christ and His Cross. That's not to say that all sermons should only be about Jesus and/or His crucifixion. But it does mean that the life and work of Christ is the *main* message that the church should preach. Further, since Jesus Christ, the Incarnation of God whom we crucified, *is* the main message of the Bible, all messages preached from God's Word should relate either directly or indirectly to Him.

So if the subject of a sermon is not related somehow to this message from God, then regardless of whatever else it might be—motivational, informative, entertaining—it is not biblical preaching. And no matter how enthusiastic or passionate the presentation, it is still the *content,* not the physical force of delivery that determines faithfulness to the message.

Modern communication theory may emphasize image and imply that what you say is not as important as how you say it, but God inspired the apostle Paul to tell the Corinthians (and us) that just the opposite is true: the message is the measure of the kind of preaching God wants you to hear. And the message of God is just what you will hear in a church where the Bible is preached, which is another reason that preaching is always relevant, and we ought to hear it.

However, you need to avoid a church where the preaching does not clearly come from the Bible. Sometimes the preacher announces a text but never really comes back to it and/or makes only passing references to any other verses from the Bible. Be wary of a sermon that does not get its shape and thrust from a verse or several verses of Scripture. (Worse yet is the "preaching" where a topic of the preacher's choice is announced—usually a current social or political issue—and the Bible is never used at all.) Often this kind of preaching is known as topical preaching. But there is an additional kind of topical preaching that takes a topic and goes all over the Bible to show what Scripture says about that topic. There is a place for this. A survey of what the Bible says about the Day of Judgment, for example, can be beneficial to all who hear.

The danger of topical preaching is that it is too easy for the preacher to determine the course of the message rather than allowing the text of Scripture to do so. Sometimes this happens because the preacher simply doesn't trust the Bible enough to let it speak its own message. Sometimes a topical sermon is the result of a man who has his own predetermined message and wants to find a Bible verse to hang it on. Although topical sermons can be biblical sermons, too often they become just a platform for the preacher to say what he wants or to speak only from the shallow well of his own experience, rather than being a mouthpiece for God's message from the text.

The kind of church you want to be a part of is one where, when the Bible is read at the beginning of the sermon, you can be confident that what follows will be built upon it. God made our hearts, and only He knows what we need most. And He made our hearts for the Word of God. Nothing nourishes us like His message. And whether or not you yet recognize it, nothing else in worship can satisfy as what God says to us.

Pastor Eric Alexander, faithful Scottish expositor of Scripture from Glasgow in the last half of the twentieth century, told this story:

> I had a young student telephone me one evening from an English city where he was at University. "I have just travelled two and a half hours by bus to the opposite side of the city," he said. "I have been here for eight weeks and have been around every church that I have been told about which is remotely evangelical. I have heard some marvelous music. I have been under some remarkably scintillating talks about current issues. I have listened to dialogue. I have seen drama and dancing. I have been witness to all kinds of excellent occasions of worship. But I am sitting back in this university residence this evening asking, 'Will nobody in this city feed my soul?' "[2]

Your soul will only be fed from the Word of God. Without it, you will be undernourished and suffer spiritual marasmus. That's what happened to a man I'll call Chris whom I spoke with not long ago. When I talked with Chris he had been in seminary for a few months and was working for a parachurch ministry that specializes in teaching the Bible and theology. Prior to enrolling in seminary, he had for several years been associate pastor in charge of drama and music at a church a couple of miles from me where the pulpit ministry was based on topical preaching aimed at people's felt needs. The church had grown from very few to hundreds in a short time.

Chris had plenty of budget money and many talented actors,

singers, musicians, and other workers as resources for his ministry. Afterward, however, he said to me, "I didn't know it when I resigned, but the following Sunday I realized that my soul was as dry and withered and empty as it could be. I had been running on the spiritual fumes of the pressure of preparation for each Sunday's drama and music. I was so busy that I hadn't realized I had dried up spiritually. It was because I was not hearing faithful, biblical exposition, but topical sermons aimed at felt needs. Everything was based upon marketing strategy. Only when I got away from all that did I realize that I was all but dead spiritually."

"Do not go," said Charles Spurgeon, the best-known preacher of the 1800s, "where it is all fine music and grand talk and beautiful architecture; those things will neither fill anybody's stomach, nor feed his soul. Go where the gospel is preached, the gospel that really feeds your soul, and go often."[3]

GOD SAVES PEOPLE THROUGH HIS MESSAGE PREACHED

You should listen to preaching in the church because the most powerful and miraculous of the works of God in the world occur through the preaching of His message. As Paul asserts in 1 Corinthians 1:21, "It pleased God through the foolishness of the message preached to save those who believe."

For this to be true doesn't necessarily mean God saves people *during* the preaching of a particular sermon, but *through* preaching. My own testimony of coming to faith in Christ is one of being saved through preaching, though my conversion did not take place during the actual presentation of the sermon. During the autumn when I was nine our church had a series of special meetings each night for a week.

On Thursday night, through the message preached, I became acutely conscious of how I had broken the laws of God and how this placed me under His eternal judgment. As I lay in bed that night, I couldn't escape the sense of alienation from God and the hopelessness of pleasing Him by doing good things. My mother came in to say good-night and sensed that something was wrong. She called my dad in, and we talked about the awareness of sin that had been awakened in me by the message that night. After my father reviewed the story of and reason for the death of Jesus, and reminded me of the offer of salvation to those who believe, there in my bed I trusted Christ to make me right with God and to give me eternal life.

So although my salvation didn't come *during* the preaching on Thursday night, it definitely came *through* it. And this is what God intends to happen through preaching in the church.

Since preaching is one of the chief ways by which God saves people, keep your distance from a church that minimizes preaching or substitutes other things for it. Whenever a church allows anything else—drama, ceremony, music, video, concert, pageant, dance—to compromise the primacy of "the message preached," it's a sign that it has lost confidence in the preaching of God's Word.

You don't need a church like this, regardless of how good its other programs are, or how many friends you have there, or how well your children like it. You need a church where you can hear the message preached.

Throughout church history, all the greatest movements of God in saving people and strengthening His church have been built upon great, God-anointed preaching. The colossal transformation in the church that occurred through the Reformers (Luther, Calvin, Zwingli, etc.) was a work of God upon souls through preaching. When the First Great Awakening blazed through England and the American Colonies, it began burning from and was sustained by the fiery pulpits of men such as Whitefield, Wesley, Edwards, Tennent, and others.

The Second Great Awakening, when the wind of God blew across America for several decades in the early 1800s, was also fundamentally the blessing of God upon preaching, preaching from men like Dwight, Finney, and Nettleton. In almost every case where large numbers of people have been converted in a concentrated period, it has been as the result of "the message preached." When the fire of God falls, the flash point is the pulpit.

An English Puritan preacher, David Clarkson, long ago described the work of God through preaching this way:

> The most wonderful things that are now done on earth are
> wrought in the public ordinances [i.e., in the elements of public
> worship, with preaching as the central element], though the com-
> monness and spiritualness of them makes them seem less
> wonderful. . . . Here the dead hear the voice of the Son of God and

His messengers, and those that hear do live. Here He gives sight to those that are born blind; it is the effect of the gospel preached to open the eyes of sinners, and to turn them from darkness to light. . . . Here He dispossesses Satan, and casts unclean spirits out of the souls of sinners that have been long possessed by them. Here He overthrows principalities and powers, vanquishes the power of darkness, and causes Satan to fall from heaven like lightning. Here He turns the whole course of nature in the souls of sinners, makes old things pass away, and all things become new. Wonders these are, and would be so accounted, were they not the common work of the public ministry. It is true indeed, the Lord has not confined himself to work these wonderful things only in public; yet the public ministry is the only ordinary means whereby He works them.[4]

Yes, you can hear preaching outside of church. And no, "the Lord has not confined himself to work" only in the church. But we should hear preaching in the church because the Lord does things through the declaration of His Word that He does not ordinarily do through other means. Since the public ministry of His Word "is the only ordinary means" whereby He does "the most wonderful things that are now done on earth," shouldn't you make listening to preaching in the church a priority?

MORE APPLICATION

Reverently and responsively listening to God's Word preached is one of the highest forms of honoring and worshiping God.

We normally think of worship as something *we* do, and since preaching is done by the preacher (and not us), many fail to think of preaching as worship. But *listening* to preaching *is* something you do, and it *is* an act of worship when you listen with an eager mind and responsive heart. The reason it is an act of *worship* is that you are listening to *God* speak (through His Word).

That's why author and theologian J. I. Packer in *The Preacher and Preaching: Reviving the Art in the Twentieth Century* states, "Congregations never honor God more than by reverently listening to His Word with a full purpose of praising and obeying Him once they see what

He has done and is doing, and what they are called to do."[5] This echoes the conviction of the great church reformer of the 1500s, Martin Luther, who wrote: "The highest worship of God is the preaching of the Word."[6]

So don't think of preaching as merely a time to learn about the Bible or to be galvanized to live more Christianly. *God* is speaking! Honor Him with your ears and soul as well as with your mouth.

It's true that you can hear much preaching on tape and by radio or TV apart from church. And I encourage you to do this, *but* as a *supplement to* and *not* a *substitute for* hearing the preaching of God's Word in person. Several reasons for this have already been given. Suffice it to say that nothing can replace the intangible interaction which passes between the preacher and listener when both have a presence in the preaching during a time of worship.

During the Persian Gulf War of 1991, a news story showed clips from the wedding of an American soldier who was stationed in Saudi Arabia and a woman who was in a church building in the United States. A satellite video link relayed the proceedings to both bride and groom, who watched each other on big-screen televisions. Yes, it was an official wedding. In fact, it was a "live" event. They even exchanged rings that had been shipped to each. But it just wasn't the same. Some things—including preaching—are simply meant to be experienced in person.

Preaching should be a primary consideration when choosing a church.

If biblical preaching is the emphasis of the pastor, it will strengthen every ministry of the church. If he sees preaching as a sideline to his calling, it will have a shallowing impact on everything else. For example, if the youth group is lively but the preaching is weak, when teenagers graduate from the youth group they may have little further interest in church (or at least the right kind of church) because the most exciting and meaningful things were only in the youth group.

There are a number of important factors to consider when choosing a church. In the last chapter I'll talk about some of the other things you should evaluate. Make *certain,* however, that you do not compromise on hearing the message preached. No ministry or program can compensate for an anemic pulpit.

During eighteen years of pastoral ministry I talked with count-less people about their search for a church home. Some wanted a large church, some wanted a small fellowship. Some wanted a good nurs-ery, others a strong children's program. Often I was told that the quali-ty of the music ministry was the top criterion.

More often than anything else, people mentioned the caliber of the youth ministry as the most critical factor in their decision of which church to join. "We want to make sure that the youth group has lots of activities and events," they would say as they knit their eyebrows with intensity. I was astonished at how often I heard, "We're going to let our children decide which church we join." I understand the impor-tance of all these things, especially when it comes to having your chil-dren in an environment that is going to shape them spiritually. But why did almost no one say to me, "I want to make sure that I and my family will hear God's Word preached faithfully"?

Remember that it is God's Word that changes hearts and lives for God, not social activities (as good and necessary as they are). It's the gospel that is the power of God unto salvation to everyone who believes (Romans 1:16), not activities and programs. God saves peo-ple through the message preached. Make sure your family will consis-tently hear what will save them and build them up.

Preachers and their preaching need your prayers.

Undoubtedly the best-known preacher of the nineteenth century was Charles Haddon Spurgeon of London. He began his ministry in 1854 at age nineteen and remained in the same pastorate until his death at age fifty-seven. Six thousand people crowded to hear him each Sunday in a day when such congregations were unheard of. Wherever he preached, the building was full. On one occasion he preached to 23,654 at the Crystal Palace (without amplification). He regularly asked church members not to attend the following Sunday so that unconverted visitors might find a seat. One Sunday in 1879, the entire building was vacated so that those who had been left outside could get a seat, and still every seat was filled. Thousands were con-verted during his ministry.

An American preacher once visited Spurgeon and was given a tour of the church building where he ministered, the Metropolitan Tabernacle. He noticed that there was no heat in the worship center, so he asked, "Don't you have a heating plant?" Spurgeon responded by leading him down to a large basement room. In that room four hundred men met before each service to pray for the pastor and the salvation of souls. Spurgeon said, "That's our heating plant."[7] He responded similarly in 1882 when some American visitors to the Tabernacle asked what was the secret of his success: "My people pray for me."[8]

Do you want better preaching? Pray for it! Pray for the preacher at your church. A prayerless church will likely get the kind of preaching for which it prays.

In contrast to Spurgeon's story I read somewhere about another well-known, nineteenth century preacher (American in this case) named T. DeWitt Talmadge. One Sunday evening he was the guest preacher at a church not far from the church he pastored in Brooklyn. In his own pulpit that morning the Lord seemed to bless his message with unusual power. But as he preached the same sermon that night his words seemed to fall to the floor as soon as they were over the pulpit.

One of his church leaders who had made the trip with him asked, "How can the same message given by the same man on the same day seem so powerful in one church and so flat in another?"

"Poor preaching," Talmadge answered, "is God's curse on a prayerless church."

Even the apostle Paul frequently requested prayer for his preaching. In fact, it's fascinating to realize that in places such as Ephesians 6:18–20 and Colossians 4:2–4, he requested prayer *not* for his unconverted listeners, but for himself and his preaching to them.

The days are long passed when preaching was the most interesting event available to people. No preacher can compete with the movies, sports events, or special effects on television. And people who have lived with a daily diet of these fast-changing, Technicolor™ images quickly develop glazed eyes like fish in a cooler if a man simply stands and starts talking about the Bible. Preaching must be prayed for, so that supernatural power is sensed by both preacher and listener.

Have you tended to think of biblical preaching as irrelevant? Maybe part of the problem is the lack of prayer support for the preaching you are hearing. "You do not have," says James 4:2, "because you do not ask."

One measurement of your spiritual health is your hunger for God's Word preached.

Spiritually robust Christians hunger for the proclamation of God's message. This is part of the nourishment God has planned for the soul, so it is healthful for you to desire it, just as it is a mark of physical health to have a good appetite.

In contrast to this, when the spiritual soundness of a church or an individual is waning, substitutes for preaching are sought. That's why we read of churches "staging drama productions *in place of* sermons." This is not to say that within the ministry of a church there is no place for drama, film, or special musical events. But a frequent desire for such things to replace the preaching of God's Word is symptomatic of spiritual infirmity.

Second Timothy 4:3–4 is a sober recognition that some people will want to replace sound, doctrinal preaching with teaching that is more entertaining: "For the time will come when they will not endure sound doctrine, but according to their own desires, because they have itching ears, they will heap up for themselves teachers; and they will turn their ears away from the truth, and be turned aside to fables." If such serious words are spoken of those who want less doctrine and more entertainment in sermons, how much more grim is the condition of those who find it hard to listen to any kind of preaching at all?

How's *your* appetite for listening to preaching in the church?

CHAPTER FIVE

WHY WORSHIP WITH THE CHURCH?

· · · · · · · ❖ · · · · · · ·

Accustomed as we are to criticizing the church,
we need to remind ourselves that God's people
are precious to Him and that He delights in their
corporate worship. As important as our private
worship is, it must be balanced by corporate worship.

Warren W. Wiersbe

I can worship God outdoors as well as I can at church."

Have you heard that line? I've heard it countless times. Just two days ago someone called and said she had been trying to talk about the things of God with a co-worker. She wasn't sure how to answer her fellow employee, who had protested, "Why do I have to go to church? I can worship God as well at home as I can there."

All my life I've heard arguments about the acceptability of worship at the golf course, the lake, in the woods, and other places. For many it's not a matter of worshiping God *as well* in nature, but *better.* Others have private "worship services" with a Bible and a tape of worship choruses, and they find such worship more satisfying than worship in the church. Perhaps you've often thought the same thing yourself. If this is true, then why worship with the church?

It is not the purpose of this chapter to contend for the general necessity and value of worshiping God. That we must worship God is plain by scriptural demand and spiritual desire. Jesus reiterated the Old Testament decree, "You shall worship the Lord your God" (Matthew 4:10). One of the last commands in the Bible is simply "Worship God" (Revelation 22:9). And surely the spirit of each one who truly knows his Maker resonates with the invitation of Psalm 95:6, "Oh come, let us worship and bow down; let us kneel before the Lord our Maker." How could anyone know the God of the Bible without worshiping Him?

Instead, this chapter is concerned with the importance and worth of worshiping God *with* His people—the church—when and where they gather to worship Him.

GOD REVEALS HIMSELF MORE CLEARLY IN CONGREGATIONAL WORSHIP THAN IN NATURE

I do not deny that we can worship God in a cathedral of sky that's bursting with light and the smells of the earth, accompanied by a chorus of sparrows. In fact, I affirm it. The skies above and the whole world around us overflow with the glory of God (Psalm 19:1; Isaiah 6:3). I agree with C. H. Spurgeon: "All places are places of worship to a Christian."[1] Wherever we go, everything in nature should prompt us to worship God, "For since the creation of the world His invisible attributes are clearly seen, being understood by the things that are made, even His eternal power and Godhead" (Romans 1:20). God has powerfully revealed Himself to us through His creation, and our spiritual eyes are shut whenever we cannot see God in His world in a way that fills us with wonder and worship.

Although God does reveal Himself in nature, He does so in a limited way. Creation, as clearly and beautifully as it reveals the Creator, is not the *clearest* revelation of God. God has revealed Himself most completely in Jesus Christ and in Scripture—much more than through creation.

So what is God like? Look at Jesus. Jesus is God, and His life and words declare the nature and will of God. As one of Jesus' closest disciples put it, "No one has seen God at any time. The only begotten Son, who is in the bosom of the Father, He has declared Him" (John 1:18).

We also know what God is like from what He has said to us. "All Scripture is given by inspiration of God," wrote the apostle Paul to Timothy, "and is profitable for doctrine, for reproof, for correction, for instruction in righteousness" (2 Timothy 3:16). The word *inspiration* means "God-breathed." The words of Scripture are out of the mouth of

God. These words are "profitable for doctrine," including the doctrine of God, that is, the nature and will and ways of God.

Here's the point: You won't hear about Christ and you won't hear the God-breathed words when you worship God in nature, but you will when you worship with the church. There is a much more conspicuous and perceptible proclamation of God in congregational worship than in nature. For example, creation reveals God as Creator, but not as Savior. And the Bible says that God's work as Savior—an action whereby He makes a "new creation" (2 Corinthians 5:17)—is more glorious than creation itself.

So it just isn't true that you can consistently worship God as well on the golf course, at the lake, in a stadium, on a hike or bike through the woods, or in the privacy of your own home or backyard as you can with His people at church. If you really want to worship God, you can never do better than worshiping Him where His Word is preached and Christ is proclaimed.

GOD IS GLORIFIED MORE IN CONGREGATIONAL WORSHIP THAN IN PRIVATE WORSHIP

When a football team wins the national championship, it gets more glory if the game is shown to millions throughout the country than if no one but you were to see it individually on closed-circuit TV. An author gets more glory if many others acclaim his book than if you alone were to read the words and praise his work. Public glory obviously brings more glory than does private glory. Likewise, God gets more glory when you worship Him with the church than when you worship Him alone.

The Lord is most glorified when His glory is most declared, not when it is hidden or private. Never will Christ be more glorified than "when He comes, in that Day, to be glorified *in His saints* and to be admired *among all* those who believe," and when "at the name of Jesus *every* knee should bow, of those in heaven, and of those on earth, and of those under the earth, and that *every* tongue should confess that Jesus Christ is Lord, to the glory of God the Father" (2 Thessalonians 1:10 and Philippians 2:10–11, italics added). Despite its deficiencies, worship in the church is more like this than is private worship, and thus it brings more glory to God.

If I tell you what a wonderful wife Caffy is, and write it for all who read this book to see, that public praise brings her more glory than if I tell her privately. This is not to minimize the importance of telling her the same when we're alone, for if I don't tell her privately, it won't mean very much to her if I say great things about her to others. That's the way it is with the public worship of God too. "There is no way," says Welsh pastor Geoffrey Thomas, "that those who neglect secret worship can know communion with God in the public services of the Lord's Day."[2] It is right to worship God both alone and with the church, but worshiping God with the church brings Him more glory.

It is very simple: greater glory is given to God when many people sincerely sing together,

> Amazing grace! how sweet the sound,
> That saved a wretch like me!

than when one person sings this testimony in private. God delights in the devotion of every individual and in each moment of private worship, but we ascribe greater glory to Him when we join our hearts and voices together in a symphony of worship.

CONGREGATIONAL WORSHIP IS MORE EDIFYING THAN PRIVATE WORSHIP

Congregational worship is more edifying for the Christian than private worship, whether that worship takes place under the stars or on a couch with an open Bible, because we receive from spiritual resources that are unavailable when alone. In the public worship of God we can experience the preaching of His Word, the spiritual gifts of Christians, the prayers of our brothers and sisters in Christ, congregational praise, fellowship, and many other things that we cannot receive in private worship.

I recognize that many Christians are in churches where the congregational worship experience often lacks depth and substance. If this describes your situation, you may wish you could say to me—perhaps through tears, perhaps through clenched teeth—"The worship at my church usually isn't edifying at all. And it is rarely more meaningful to me than when I worship God privately."

Still, the *potential* is *always* present in congregational worship for greater edification than you could receive from private worship. Even in those churches where the Sunday morning ministry is of the flippant/entertainment variety or the dry/stiff sort, there are many opportunities for unanticipated breakthroughs by the Holy Spirit. Something from the sermon may be surprisingly nourishing to your soul. The words of a hymn, solo, or choral piece may strike you with unusual force. Someone may pray for you, or you may hear a prayer that conveys to God something in your own heart that has been longing for expression. The preacher, or a friend, or someone leading in worship, may be God's mouthpiece to say a word of encouragement or direction just for you. These are blessings you forfeit by absence from church.

Others Are Edified

Also, your participation in congregational worship is more edifying to *others* than if you were to worship God only by yourself. You can minister to people in ways you certainly cannot if you are not with them. We are urged in Hebrews 10:24, "And let us consider one another in order to stir up love and good works." There is a "stirring up" to "love and good works" and an opportunity for "exhorting one another" that comes from assembling for worship with other believers that cannot happen individually.

Your faithful and wholehearted involvement in the worship of God at church can influence people in ways you would never imagine. Children learn from your example. Teenagers observe Christian maturity in action. Backsliders are admonished to return to biblical priorities. Hypocrites are reproved by sincere commitment and worship.

Even the unconverted may be convicted by your involvement in public worship. The apostle Paul described such a scenario for the Corinthian church: "But if all prophesy, and an unbeliever or an uninformed person comes in, he is convinced by all, he is convicted by all. And thus the secrets of his heart are revealed; and so, falling down on his face, he will worship God and report that God is truly among you" (1 Corinthians 14:24–25).

Unbelievers Can Perceive God's Presence

Similar experiences happen throughout the world every Sunday. Before we married, Caffy was in a worship service one Lord's Day when a woman in her twenties came in as the people were singing praise to God. She was the daughter of a New York streetwalker and had for years been a drug-addicted prostitute there herself. Hooking and hitchhiking her way across the country, she had come to Fayetteville, Arkansas, and was walking past the church. She had never been in a church before but decided to go in.

Later she told Caffy that she immediately sensed what seemed to be the presence of God among the people. Falling on her face, she crawled to the front of the church, sobbing uncontrollably. People gathered around her and began to pray for her, and as she heard the gospel of Jesus she repented and believed in Him for the forgiveness of her sins. Would that have happened if she had walked past someone worshiping God privately? Countless times when I was a pastor, visitors told me that they became aware that "God was in this place" as they walked into our worship service. Never have I heard anyone say that as they watched people worship on a golf course or a lake.

Maybe you are still convinced that in your situation you get a great deal more out of private worship than public. Ask yourself, *Where can I do the most good?* Worshiping God with others ministers not only to yourself but to those around you as well. This is considering others as more important than yourself (Philippians 2:3–4), and that is like Christ.

GOD CAN BE EXPERIENCED IN UNIQUE WAYS IN CONGREGATIONAL WORSHIP

The Bible says that each believer in Christ is a temple of the Holy Spirit (1 Corinthians 6:19). This means that the Spirit of God Himself has come to live within you and made you, as a temple, a place of worship. You don't have to *go* to a temple to worship God; you *are* His temple. That's why private worship—true worship—can happen wherever you are, and why it can be so blessed.

Therefore let me affirm again that the Christian can worship God anywhere and without the assistance or presence of anyone else. You can exult in God under the stars, or at sunset, or in the mountains, or under some other canopy of creation. Christian, since your body is a temple of the Holy Spirit, the experience of worshiping God in the intimacy of privacy with Him can result in divine encounters that might never be duplicated in a congregational setting.

Conversely, it's also true that God will manifest His presence to you in congregational worship in ways you can never know even in the most glorious secret worship. That's because you are not only a temple of God as an individual, but the Bible also says (and far more often) that Christians *collectively* are God's temple. Notice the following verses that teach that the temple of God consists of the gathered people of God. That these references mean the collected church is made more clear in the Greek of the original text, because each time the word *you* is used here it is in the plural (as in "you all"), referring to the *entire* church in that locality.

- You are God's field, *you are God's building.* (1 Corinthians 3:9b)

- Do you not know that *you are the temple of God* and that the Spirit of God dwells in you? If anyone defiles the temple of God, God will destroy him. For the temple of God is holy, *which temple you are.* (1 Corinthians 3:16–17)

- For *you are the temple of the living God.* (2 Corinthians 6:16b)

- Now, therefore, you are no longer strangers and foreigners, but fellow citizens with the saints and members of the household of God, having been built on the foundation of the apostles and prophets, Jesus Christ Himself being the chief cornerstone, in whom *the whole building*, being fitted together, grows into *a holy temple* in the Lord, in whom you also are being *built together for a dwelling place of God in the Spirit.* (Ephesians 2:19–22)

- You also, as living stones, are being built up *a spiritual house.* (1 Peter 2:5a)

In the days of the Old Testament, God ordained that people build a stone-and-mortar building where He was to be worshiped. But that structure was destroyed within two generations after Jesus' ascension into heaven because God had made His own temple in the flesh and blood of His people. Today we may rightly point to each individual Christian and say "the temple of the Holy Spirit." But we must also look at our local *community* of believers and declare with equal conviction "the temple of the Holy Spirit." And there are experiences with God that can be known only when you worship within that "spiritual house."

God manifests His presence in different ways to the "living stones" of His temple when they are gathered than He does to them when they are apart.

JESUS REGULARLY PARTICIPATED IN CONGREGATIONAL WORSHIP

Jesus Christ is not only our Lord, but our example. What was His example in this matter? He faithfully participated in the congregational worship of God as practiced in His day. Luke tells us of Jesus' public worship habit: "So He came to Nazareth, where He had been brought up. And *as His custom was,* He went into the synagogue on the Sabbath day, and stood up to read" (Luke 4:16, italics added).

How can anyone claim to follow Jesus who won't worship God as Jesus did? As Jesus customarily worshiped with God's people, so should we.

CONGREGATIONAL WORSHIP IS MORE LIKE HEAVEN

Nothing you do on a consistent basis is more like the activity of heaven than worshiping God with His people. In congregational worship we express our unity with all true Christians of all time everywhere.

Observe the description in Hebrews 12:22–24 of the unity between Christians on earth with the angels and people of God in heaven: "But you have come to Mount Zion and to the city of the living God, the heavenly Jerusalem, to an innumerable company of angels, to the general assembly and church of the firstborn who are registered in heaven, to God the Judge of all, to the spirits of just men made perfect, to Jesus the Mediator of the new covenant." Through the work of Christ, we Christians on earth have spiritual access into heaven itself and to "God the Judge of all."

Like worshipers in the same room, yet divided by a veil, when we worship God there is a real sense in which we are participating in the unseen heavenly worship already occurring. Think of that. The point is that the worship in heaven, both that which is currently in process and that which will continue throughout eternity, is *congregational* worship. Thus our congregational worship is more like heaven than individual worship. Moreover, the Bible gives no indication of private worship in heaven. If you want heaven to be your eternal home, don't you want to frequently experience that which is the "nearest resemblance of heaven" on earth?

"So then," says the best-known Bible commentator, Matthew Henry, "let every saint praise him, but especially the *congregation* of saints; when they come together, let them join in praising God. The more the better; it is the more like heaven" (italics added).[3]

LEARNING TO WORSHIP WITH THE CHURCH

What if congregational worship has usually seemed inferior to private worship in your experience, even though the Bible is preached and hymns are sung in your church?

Earlier I addressed the difficulty of many Christians who believe that they are in churches that are so shallow that their private worship is consistently superior to their experience in congregational worship. But what about those Christians who have difficulties with public worship even though they are in churches where both the preaching and music are clearly biblically based?

You should evaluate your experience by the Word of God, not vice versa.

If the Bible says that these things are true about congregational worship:

- God reveals Himself more clearly in public worship than in nature,

- God is more glorified in congregational worship than in private worship,

- congregational worship is more edifying to you and others than solo worship,

- God can be experienced in church worship in ways that He cannot in solitary worship, and

- congregational worship is more like heaven than any other regular experience on earth,

then by faith you should affirm that they *are* true even if they contradict your experience. With many scriptural declarations, you must believe them before you can experience them. Will you believe in the priority of congregational worship over private worship and commit to attending public worship?

You may sometimes experience the enjoyment of God more in private worship than congregational worship.

I haven't intended to imply that every church worship service will seem more filled with God than any time of private worship. That will not be true.

One of my most memorable encounters with God occurred in September of 1985. A group from our church was part of a larger team of Americans invited by Swedish Baptists to do evangelistic work in their country. A couple of hours before I was to preach one night, I walked half a mile to a football-field-sized lake. The leaves were heavy on the trees that stood on guard all around the shore. Autumn had burnished them to russet and gold. Wispy fingers of clouds nudged the sun toward its westerly resting place, and it responded by tinting them with deep, restful shades of orange, violet, and mauve.

Not a ripple disturbed the lake. When a leaf fell from its twig and twirled slowly toward the water it rested—flat, sodden, and still—exactly where it fell. The surface was absolutely placid. The liquid mirror below reflected the iridescence of the glowing sunset and the leafy gold. The air was even calmer than the water, and yet it was so cool and clear that no breeze was needed. The motionless silence of the scene was mesmerizing. Everything I could see testified to the creativity of God, the glory of God, and the peace of God.

How astonishing heaven must be if it is more glorious than this, I thought.

Praise You, Father, for making such a beautiful world.

In heaven I will experience this kind of serenity forever.

Thank You, Lord Jesus, for giving me peace with God, which means infinitely more to me than temporary tranquillity.

Such unforgettable moments alone with God are more precious

than many group worship experiences, but in treasuring them we must not minimize the priority of enjoying God in congregational worship.

You have not been thoughtful or wholehearted in congregational worship if this inability to worship publicly is typical.

If the Bible is preached and the music is doctrinally sound at your church, and yet you consistently find yourself unable to enjoy God there, either you have not been thoughtful or you have not been wholehearted about what you have heard and sung. You cannot be mentally passive in church and expect to meet God. If the Word of God is proclaimed from the pulpit and the truth of God is declared in the music, then the banquet of worship is set. But you must think about what you hear and engage your heart if you are going to be nourished by the spiritual food.

Recently I heard a pastor of a church in a very conservative denomination tell of a difficulty he was experiencing because he taught the deity of Christ. Although this is a foundational belief in that denomination, somehow this church was an anomaly. An old deacon, who was one of the people angry about the doctrine, had told the pastor that in eighty years of attending the church he had never heard it taught that Jesus is God.

Well, I must admit to some skepticism about the deacon's claim. But even if the church has had a succession of liberal pastors who denied Jesus' deity, surely "Hark! The Herald Angels Sing" has been part of their worship at Christmas, and therefore he has almost certainly sung the words "Veiled in flesh the Godhead see;/ Hail the incarnate Deity!" So it's probably not that the doctrine of Jesus' deity has never been taught there, but rather that this man hadn't been thinking about what he has heard and sung.

However, it's just as easy for believers with orthodox doctrine to be singing, "I love You, Lord" while thinking, *I wonder how much longer the service will last,* or, *Who is that sitting with the Smiths today?* We may miss much in worship—including the presence of God—if we aren't mindful of what we do so that we can do it with all our hearts. We must be aware of what we are saying and doing if we want to avoid taking the Lord's name in vain (that is, addressing Him in prayer or song without thinking of Him) and if we want actual worship in our acts of worship.

Most often you must *seek* God in public worship in order to find Him. You enjoy God more in private worship because the nature of private worship requires that you take initiative. In meaningful daily worship you have to consider the words of Scripture as your eyes pass over them, prayer requires thought and summons emotions, and so forth. But in congregational worship it is easy to sit back and simply observe, waiting for a spiritual jolt.

Realize that you must take the same initiative in congregational worship that you do in private worship if you expect to recognize the presence of God there. For if the Bible is being preached and the music is doctrinally sound at your church, more than enough is there to stir your heart if you are paying attention.

Congregational worship surpasses private worship, but it does not replace it.

Although I have primarily addressed those who think public worship is virtually optional (especially if they have an enriching daily devotional life), my experience indicates that there are many more people who have almost no private worship at all even though they attend church every Sunday. If you fall into this category, it would be easy for you to think that your faithfulness in corporate worship attendance is sufficient for Christian maturity. Remember, God manifests Himself through *private* worship in ways you will *never* experience in church. As Matthew Henry put it, "Public worship will not excuse us from secret worship."[4]

If you love God, how can you neglect worship in the church?

Congregational worship is ordained by God. He has chosen worship in the church as a place of special communion between Him and His people. He takes pleasure in meeting you there. He wants you to enjoy Him there. How can your conscience—and your *heart*—allow you to refuse? Believe these closing words about congregational worship from David Clarkson:

> Here is the sweetest enjoyment of God, the clearest discoveries of his glory, the powerful workings of the Spirit, the precious blood of Christ in its force and efficacy, the exceeding great and precious promises in their sweetest influences, spiritual life and

strength, soul comforts and refreshments, the conversion of sinners, the edification of the body of Christ, the salvation of souls. . . . Here the Lord, if anywhere in the world, receives the glory due unto his name, Ps. xxix. 1, 2. To worship God in public is the way to give him the glory due to his name; and is not this of highest value? It is your glory too.[5]

CHAPTER SIX

WHY WITNESS WITH THE CHURCH?

· · · · · · · · ❧ · · · · · · · ·

The New Testament knows
nothing of free-lance Christianity.
It is the corporate witness of the redeemed
fellowship that is used by the Spirit of God.

Geoffrey King

This is an ancient story, but true. Around three thousand years ago, four men were banished from the city of Samaria because they had leprosy. Although the people of the city had removed the diseased men from their midst, the city wasn't much safer because of it. A huge army from Syria had besieged it. The siege had lasted so long that the people of Samaria were near the point of mass starvation. In their hunger, some had even resorted to cannibalism.

With the "valued" people inside the walled city starving, you can imagine how little these social outcasts had to eat. Considering their options, one said, "Look, we've got to do something. Even if we found a way to get back into the city we would soon die there of hunger. If we continue sitting outside the gate of a starving city we will starve too. Why not go to the Syrians and see if they will give us food? If they kill us—well, we would have died in a matter of days anyway. Who knows, they might feed us and let us live."

And so, as the sun set, four gaunt lepers limped toward the Syrian camp. At first they were surprised that no sentry shouted for them to halt. They must have wondered if they had caught a soldier shirking his duty or if the Syrians were so overconfident of their advantage that they left a camp entrance unguarded. But as they kept walking into the

Syrian positions, there was no sign of *any* soldier.

The Bible explains in 2 Kings 7:6–7, "For the Lord had caused the army of the Syrians to hear the noise of chariots and the noise of horses—the noise of a great army; so they said to one another, 'Look, the king of Israel has hired against us the kings of the Hittites and the kings of the Egyptians to attack us!' Therefore they arose and fled at twilight, and left the camp intact—their tents, their horses, and their donkeys—and they fled for their lives."

Timidly, the men walked into the camp wondering if death awaited them. Instead they found unattended campfires cooking their supper. Food! Everywhere was food! They didn't go all through the camp searching for signs of soldiers. According to the next verse, they were so hungry that "when these lepers came to the outskirts of the camp, they went into one tent and ate and drank, and carried from it silver and gold and clothing, and went and hid them; then they came back and entered another tent, and carried some from there also, and went and hid it" (v. 8).

By now it was quite dark, and the newly energetic quartet found itself faced with a question. Should the men enjoy themselves—feasting on the food, celebrating their fortune, enjoying the fellowship of their intimate group, and fantasizing about their fabulous new future—or should they share the good news with those who had despised them?

Their dilemma is our dilemma as Christians. We have feasted on the gospel of Jesus Christ and found food that gives us eternal life. We have a joy in God and a depth of relationships with God's people that others do not have. We have a future that is beyond description or human comprehension, and it's guaranteed by God Himself. There's more than enough, and all that we have is available to everyone. And yet, it's easy to simply enjoy our individual comforts instead of working together to tell others the Good News that their souls don't have to starve.

Evangelism sounds like a noble idea, but why don't we just leave it to those who have the gifts or the time to go to the trouble of going back to tell the others? Why not leave it up to each individual to witness in his own way when he can? Why should we participate in outreach efforts with others from our local fellowship? Why should we feel burdened to start or strengthen an evangelistic ministry of our church?

GOD IS GLORIFIED MORE THROUGH
A CONGREGATIONAL WITNESS

It brings more glory to God when we bear witness of Him together than when we do so individually. Now, this is not to minimize one-on-one evangelism. As individuals we should take advantage of every opportunity to tell the message about Jesus Christ. I don't want to *de*-emphasize personal evangelism; I want to highlight what has been neglected, namely, congregational and small group evangelism.

The broader the testimony, the more God is glorified. Notice why the writer of Psalm 96 says we should tell the whole world about Him: "Declare His glory among the nations, His wonders among all peoples. For the Lord is great and greatly to be praised" (3–4a). A congregation of believers praising God can give greater praise than can one person. An assembly can give glory to God with greater volume (which the Hebrew word translated *greatly* sometimes means) and variety than any individual can.

Let's see this applied in the matter of congregational versus individual evangelism. Suppose you participate in an outreach group. This group could be part of an organized ministry of the church or a cluster of friends who eat or play together regularly and try to invite unbelievers. There might be a dozen or more or less than half that many. As you gather one night there's at least one non-Christian friend there. An opportunity arises and those in the group talk about how they met Christ and what He has done in their lives.

One tells of being raised in a Christian home and coming to faith through a parent's influence, while another speaks of having never been in church or hearing the Bible until a stranger told him about Jesus. One speaks of being led to Christ by a close friend or pastor. Another says the key factor was a Christian book, and still another points to the influence of a Bible study. One speaks of experiencing God's grace after trying to earn her way into heaven by being good or keeping religious rules, but another describes his life before Christ as attempting to live without any moral limits whatsoever. In the midst of these testimonies, you tell your own story of becoming a follower of Jesus.

As everyone in this group effort identifies with the same Lord and Savior, He is presented as the God for everyone and as a God who can save anyone. Greater glory is thus given to God through the *variety* than if the non-Christian were to hear only of your experience.

This "glory multiplication" principle that exists when a small group witnesses together extends also to the entire local church fellowship. When all the members of the church body come together to evangelize collectively, God is more greatly glorified than when they witness on their own. Far more gifts, talents, and insights contribute to the outreach than anyone could muster alone.

Last night I attended a church's Christmas program, designed exclusively as a community outreach event. An orchestra, choir, and dramatic cast combined to tell the story of the birth, death, and resurrection of Jesus. Skillfully done, but without world-imitating glitz, the work of these four hundred people uplifted Christ and glorified God in a way I could never expect to do by myself.

Not least in the consideration of God getting greater glory in congregational evangelism than in personal evangelism is the demonstration of *unity*. Jesus said that the world would not believe our message without Christian unity. In John 17:20–21 He asked the Father for those "who will believe in Me through their word; that they all may be one . . . that the world may believe that You sent Me." Further, from the first verse of this chapter to the last paragraph, the theme of the glory of God is woven throughout.

The connection is this: In a world where everyone has broken relationships, supernatural unity in a church family bears witness to the power of the gospel in a marvelously God-glorifying manner. And as necessary as individual witnessing is, it can never show unity as a congregational witness can. Or, to put it another way, Jesus said that *unity was essential for effective evangelism, and it takes a* group *of Christians to demonstrate unity.* Therefore churches need to consider ways to exhibit unity in the presence of unbelievers, for this both brings glory to God and brings people to Christ.

For the glory of God, find a way to be personally involved with others in the outreach of your church.

THERE IS JOY IN HAVING A PART IN SOMEONE COMING TO CHRIST

In Acts 15:3, Paul and Barnabas were traveling from Antioch 350 miles south to Jerusalem. As they journeyed, they told the churches along the way about the response to the gospel they had seen in their missionary work: "They passed through Phoenicia and Samaria, describing the conversion of the Gentiles; and they caused great joy to all the brethren." In all likelihood one of the reasons the people rejoiced in this report was that they had prayed for Paul and Barnabas and perhaps had supported them in other ways. So part of their great joy in the news of the conversion of the Gentiles came from thinking, *We had a part in their conversion.* Even though they weren't the actual spokesmen, they shared in the joy in seeing others come to Christ because they shared in the labor.

Today we would refer to such a meeting as a missionary report. Most churches have them in one form or another. Missionaries come home and report to those who support them about what God has done on the mission field. I cannot overemphasize the importance of prayerfully and financially supporting those who go to the home and foreign mission fields. And those who hold the ropes for missionaries, as did the Christians in Acts 15:3, can know the same kind of joy as these givers and pray-ers who heard the report of Paul and Barnabas.

Join an Evangelistic Group from Your Church

However, those who are involved in their church's *local* outreach ministry can experience even *more immediately and directly* the joy of having a part in seeing someone come to Christ. Have you been privileged to lead someone to faith in Jesus? Sadly, only a small fraction of evangelicals has. A friend who is a professor of evangelism confirmed what I've often heard, that only 5 percent of those in one of America's most evangelistic denominations (so it's probably true in most groups) have ever led another to Christ. But it doesn't have to be that way, even if you aren't confident in your personal evangelism skills.

By participating in one or more of the various means of outreach of your church, you can be part of an evangelistic *group* that presents the gospel as a team effort. When someone is converted, the joy is shared by all who share in the witness.

Perform Evangelistic Service with Your Church

Here's an example. A few years ago in the church I pastored in suburban Chicago, a member of a women's Sunday school class met a handicapped man through her volunteer work. Amrind had narrowly escaped from Cambodia with his wife after the Communists had over-run their country. History has reported on the millions killed by the new regime, and among them were Amrind's parents and siblings. After living briefly in California and Pennsylvania, Amrind made his way to Chicago. Eventually his photographic skills and willingness to work resulted in a good job with a photo lab in the city.

For the first time in years, Amrind had a sense of stability and security for his family, which now included two young sons. But one tragic night, in an event as cruel as any they had escaped in Cambodia, their lives changed forever. Amrind was mugged in an elevator, shot, and left a quadriplegic. After his wounds healed, he was taken to a rehabilitation hospital west of Chicago in Wheaton. It was there he met the woman from our church.

When she told her Sunday school class about Amrind and his family's needs, they began a schedule of visiting and ministering to them. Nara, Amrind's wife, could not drive. Women from the class took her to apply for assistance, to get groceries and medicine, and to run other errands. Clothes and school supplies were bought for the boys.

Before long the women of the class asked me to call on Amrind and his family. I did so, and after a few visits of explaining the gospel and conversing with them about the Bible, both Amrind and Nara gave their lives to Christ. I continued to meet with them regularly, and so did others who helped them with Bible study and discipleship. As you can imagine, when word spread of their conversion, there were many whose joy was as great as mine. For even though I had been the one to discuss the gospel with them at length and to pray with them when they confessed their faith in Jesus, every woman in that Sunday school class and many other people in our church had been part of the overall witness to this family.

Whether the effort is churchwide or by a small group, whether it's part of an ongoing program of the church, a short-term ministry, or a one-time event, everybody can do something in a group of people that witnesses.

GOD HAS CHOSEN THE LOCAL CHURCH AS THE PRIMARY CHANNEL FOR HIS MESSAGE

When writing instructions to his young pastor friend, Timothy, the apostle Paul gave a God-inspired description of the church in 1 Timothy 3:15, "I write so that you may know how you ought to conduct yourself in the house of God, which is *the church* of the living God, *the pillar and ground of the truth*" (italics added). The truth of God is built upon and upheld by the church.

The church is God's earthly steward for the gospel. Although this has application to the church as a whole, it finds its daily expression in the local church. There is no single, worldwide voice for the church. It is to individual churches that the truth, God's message to the world, is entrusted for proclamation. As part of a local church, you have the responsibility to help it fulfill its commission.

This verse prompts me to say that evangelism is not only our job as individual Christians, it is also our task *with* other Christians. Although we may be scattered throughout the week in such ways that we rarely see another believer, we are not lone scouts for the church in enemy territory. We are part of a great army, and sometimes we need to go into the world *together*.

Because the local church is the primary channel for God's message in the world, you shouldn't let involvement in a parachurch ministry keep you from witnessing for Christ through your church. I would broadly define a parachurch organization as a Christian organization that is not a church or part of a church. There are many such outstanding ministries, and I would not discourage you from supporting some of them. Still, the church is the only organization established by Jesus Christ and only it—"the church of the living God"—is "the pillar and ground of the truth." Christians should give their primary support to their local churches, and then, as time and money permit, assist parachurch organizations.

Parachurch ministries typically have one emphasis—Bible study, missions, literature, student work, discipleship, etc. Because they focus on one thing, they usually do it better than most churches. This effectiveness attracts (and deserves) support. And yet, we must not forget that the local church, which necessarily must perform a broad spectrum of ministries and can't afford the luxury of much specialization, remains God's primary channel for the gospel.

With all its flaws, God has not given up on the church, and He never will. So don't *you* abandon the local church and its ministries. And don't assume that it can't minister in a particular area as well as a parachurch organization. What the church needs are men and women who will be as committed to its ministries as others are to parachurch ministries, especially in the areas of outreach and evangelism.

EVANGELISM IS THE PRIVILEGE AND RESPONSIBILITY OF EVERYONE IN THE CHURCH

Let's look at a verse written by one of the apostles and intended for all Christians: "But you are a chosen generation, a royal priesthood, a holy nation, His own special people, that you may proclaim the praises of Him who called you out of darkness into His marvelous light" (1 Peter 2:9). Peter portrays the church of God four ways here:

- a chosen generation
- a royal priesthood
- a holy nation
- His own special people

Too often this is all that's emphasized from this verse. But don't miss the *purpose* given here for God's people: "*that* you may proclaim the praises of Him who called you out of darkness into His marvelous light." One of the purposes for which God made the church was so that she would proclaim Him. That includes what we call evangelism.

In the next chapter the privilege and responsibility of all Christians to witness is even plainer: "But sanctify the Lord God in your hearts, and always be ready to give a defense to everyone who asks you a reason for the hope that is in you, with meekness and fear" (1 Peter 3:15). If someone asks you why you believe in the Lord, you are to be ready to answer. This is expected of every believer, regardless of spiritual age or experience. Granted, this verse refers to when anyone *asks* about your faith; nevertheless, this readiness to testify is the assignment for each of Jesus' followers without exception.

I attended a ministers' conference where a well-known pastor told a story about his first church. It was obvious that the church was weak in evangelism. So he announced that on Sunday nights he would teach how to witness to others about Christ. Delighted by the turnout, he assumed that the people were eager to learn how to communicate their faith. About halfway through the first session, one of the church leaders raised his hand.

"Pastor, why are you teaching us this?"

He was dumbfounded by a question that called for such an obvious answer. With eyes and palms opened wide, he finally explained, "So that you can share the gospel and lead people to Christ."

"No sir," came the sharp-edged reply, "that's what we pay *you* for."

Anyone who thinks that talking about Jesus is a mercenary duty for a professional rather than the inestimable privilege of every Christian doesn't understand the gospel. Evangelism is not just something we're *told* to do, but something we *get* to do. As members of the church of Christ we have the honor of being royal ambassadors. Each one of us gets to tell the world the truth about the Creator of the universe, the awesome majesty of His holiness, the greatness of His love in sending His Son, and the glory of His heavenly home. And then we have the authority to invite people to know Him. Who could truly understand what a blessing this Christian birthright is and then speak of paying someone to do it in the same way you'd speak of paying someone to haul away your garbage?

Perhaps the reason that some have such a negative perception of evangelism is that they can only imagine it as an individual event. Witnessing, in their mind, means either going alone door-to-door or buttonholing strangers in a public place. They've never realized that evangelism can be a natural and enjoyable experience or that they can be a part of a group that witnesses as a team.

Think about it: If sharing the gospel is the privilege and responsibility of *everyone* in the church, then the people in the church ought to do at least some evangelism *together*. Where's the evangelistic place in the church for you?

TOGETHER WE CAN DEMONSTRATE THE REALITY OF CHRIST'S POWER AND LOVE BETTER

Earlier I mentioned that unity, which Jesus said was necessary so "that the world may believe" (John 17:21), cannot be demonstrated by an individual witness. In the same way, the reality of Christ's power and love can be visible in a *group* of Christians in ways that cannot be seen in a solitary believer. Jesus describes this in John 13:35, "By this all will know that you are My disciples, if you have love for one another." Francis Schaeffer called the love of Christians for each other the ultimate answer or "the final apologetic" we can give to the world. In his words, "we must never forget that the final apologetic which Jesus gives us is the observable love of true Christians for true Christians."[1]

Showing love for one another obviously requires the presence of other Christians. And loving other believers so that "all will know that you are [Jesus'] disciples" means showing love to them in ways that unbelievers perceive. So to fulfill this verse in real life it will sometimes be necessary for Christians to show love to one another *while* non-Christians are around. One of the best and most consistent ways this can be done is for members of a church to *organize* themselves for this purpose. Do ministries already exist at your church where Christians can show love to each other in the presence of non-Christians? These might exist in the form of care groups of various types, service groups, outreach groups, men's or women's ministries, senior adult ministries, singles ministries, and so forth. If your church has them, then find a way to join one. If not, start one.

A Group That Loves One Another

Christian love is something unbelievers don't see in the world. They may see loving *individuals* from time to time, but not a loving group. In fact, they may see very few *families* in which everyone seems to love each other, much less a larger group of people. And when they do see real love in action, it gets their attention just as Jesus promised it would. There is a unique power that accompanies a witness to Christ by a group of people who show that they love one another.

Author Will Metzger echoes: "When Christians as a group get together, there is power. The Scriptures say that others shall know we are Christ's disciples by the love we display for each other. We should welcome unbelievers as observers in our fellowship communities where we speak not mere words but live concepts. Our brother-sister relationships are the dynamic equivalents for the truth we wish to convey."[2]

The phenomenal growth of the Jerusalem church in the book of Acts is attributed precisely to God's blessing on its powerful and loving congregational witness:

> Now all who believed were together, and had all things in com-
> mon, and sold their possessions and goods, and divided them
> among all, as anyone had need. So continuing daily with one
> accord in the temple, and breaking bread from house to house,
> they ate their food with gladness and simplicity of heart, praising
> God and having favor with all the people. And the Lord added to
> the church daily those who were being saved. (Acts 2:44–47)

Notice specifically the things done collectively, the corporate nature of their activity. They had a life together that became a theater for their love. And as a result people were being saved.

The church was still capturing the attention of the world with its uncommon love 150 years later. Tertullian, an early father of the church, wrote his famous *Apology* to Roman magistrates defending Christians against slanderous charges and demanding for them the same due process of law given to other citizens. In it he noted the impact on unbelievers by love within the church: "But it is mainly the deeds of a love so noble that lead many to put a brand upon us. 'See,' they say, 'how they love one another.' "[3] A conspicuous, congregational love in a loveless world will not be ignored.

The Testimony of a Loving Group

When, as an individual Christian, you show love to an unbeliever (which each of us ought to do), he can always excuse you as an exception. But when he sees several Christians treating each other and him with love, the power of such concurrent Christianity is much more undeniable. It's easy for someone to think you're just a "religious fanatic" when you speak privately of your faith. But it's more difficult to discount the testimony of an entire group that makes the same claims about the love and power of God. "They can shrug off one Christian 'kook,'" says Will Metzger, "but when they continue to meet more, it starts them thinking!"[4] Do you meet with Christians around non-Christians in ways that start the unbelievers thinking?

I know a man who was born again when he was seventy. In the half-dozen years before his conversion, his five adult children and two of their spouses became Christians. Not long ago I heard him say to some of them, "I realized that you had something I didn't." Although the family had always been close, he had seen a change in the way they related to each other and to those from their church. Frequently he went with them to worship, and he was often around in their homes when one of them hosted a group from church. He was loved by the people in the church, and he noticed the loving difference in them and his children. Eventually this caused him to rethink his own claims to faith and to recognize that he wasn't a Christian.

The key to reaching this man wasn't the testimony of one bold, articulate witness, but the cumulative impact of seeing Christ in many people. It's testimonies such as this that prompt Metzger to make this revolutionary but thought-worthy statement: "Indeed, it is questionable if evangelism can be done at all without reference to a Christian community."[5] Yet how much evangelism is attempted today without a single thought to a Christian community? We need to recover the evangelistic power of loving relationships. Ask yourself, "How can I be part of a group showing unity and love in ways that non-Christians can see?"

JUDGMENT IS COMING AND PEOPLE MUST BE PERSUADED BY THE GOSPEL

In preparing for evangelism, we should never forget sobering passages such as 2 Corinthians 5:10–11: "For we must all appear before the judgment seat of Christ, that each one may receive the things done in the body, according to what he has done, whether good or bad. Knowing, therefore, the terror of the Lord, we persuade men." Because we know of "the terror of the Lord" that awaits the unconverted at the judgment seat of Christ, "we persuade men." That is, we plead with people, "Come to Christ. Judgment is coming. Heaven and hell are real." And since the verse reads "we [plural] persuade men," that includes a congregational persuasion as well as persuasion by a collection of individuals.

L. R. Scarborough, president of Southwestern Baptist Theological Seminary in the early part of the 1900s, said that if we could only have a five-minute glimpse into hell our evangelism would be changed for a lifetime. I've tried to imagine what a look into hell would be like. Afterward, I'm sure the "terror of the Lord" would take on a dreadful new meaning, and we would plead with people to come to Christ with more urgent persuasion than ever before.

You haven't had that five-minute look, but do you believe that hell is real? Do you believe that people who die without Christ are going there? What are you doing about it? One thing you can do is become involved with an outreach ministry of your church. Even though you may have little confidence in your personal evangelism proficiency, you can be part of a group that purposes together in various ways to persuade men with the gospel of Jesus Christ.

APPLYING THE TRUTHS OF SCRIPTURE

Are you passive or are you passionate about reaching the lost through your church?

Are you complacent or are you convicted about helping to reach those who are, as you once were, outside of Christ? If you are content to come to church on Sundays, be fed spiritually, and never participate in any ministry that sees someone come to Christ, then you don't have the heart of Jesus for the lost. Are you *un*evangelistic and unconcerned about it? If so, you need to repent and to remember the last earthly words of Jesus (Matthew 28:19–20).

What can you do to strengthen the witness of your church?

It's impossible to list all the options, but let me make a few brief suggestions.

When was the last time you brought someone to hear the preaching of God's Word in the context of sincere, corporate worship? I've found that the longer someone has been a churchgoer, the less likely he or she is to invite a lost person to church. If that has happened to you, think of someone you could invite to join you next Sunday.

Talk to your pastor or another church leader about hosting a home evangelism meeting where you can assist in a gospel witness even though you may not be the mouthpiece. Invite guests who have questions about God, Christianity, and the Bible to come and ask their questions of a "Bible expert." Tell them that the speaker will first give an overview of the Bible as a platform for questions, then they can ask any and all sincere questions. I've met many who feel incapable of speaking in such a meeting but are willing to open their homes for one.

Could you participate in a regular prayer meeting for the conversion of the lost?

Ask your pastor or outreach leader to tell you about opportunities in the ongoing evangelism ministries at the church. There are always plenty to choose from for someone who genuinely wants to play a part in seeing people come to know Jesus Christ.

Remember the four starving lepers of Samaria who walked into the deserted camp of the enemy? Surprised by God with food and a future, they knew they couldn't keep their wonderful discovery to themselves. The Bible reports that they said to one another, "We are not doing right. This day is a day of good news, and we remain silent" (2 Kings 7:9). So they did something about their passivity. *Together* they went and told others the good news. Are you willing to do as they did?

CHAPTER SEVEN

WHY SERVE IN CHURCH?

· · · · · · · · · ❖ · · · · · · · ·

So many people today are not looking for a
place to serve, but for a place to be served.
That's normal for the world to have that attitude,
but we are very alarmed and concerned to see
this attitude among Christians.

Letter from a woman in Ohio to
Focus on the Family editor Rolf Zettersten

Sunday, December 7, 1941, in the words of President Franklin D.
Roosevelt, "is a date that will live in infamy." At 7:50 that morning, a
strike force from the empire of Japan launched an aerial attack on
Pearl Harbor, Hawaii, the operating base of the U.S. Pacific fleet.
Eighteen ships were hit and two hundred aircraft were destroyed or
damaged. At least 2,400 Americans were killed and 1,300 wounded.

The bombs and torpedoes caught the American forces completely
by surprise. As a result of months of meticulous planning and practice,
the Japanese scored a brilliant tactical victory. In less than two hours it
appeared that they had crippled U.S. naval power in the Pacific.

But the raid proved to be a colossal blunder politically and psy-
chologically. Overnight, America went from a somewhat unconcerned
country trying to stay out of the war to a unified nation intent on winning it. All over the land on Monday morning there were long lines at
recruiting offices. Volunteers rushed to join the armed forces without a
second thought to their plans for the future. Tens of thousands reported
late to work or school that morning only to say that they'd be leaving
for boot camp in a few days. Teenagers and middle-aged men alike
lied about their age and physical condition in order to put on the uni-
form. Grown men wept when they were told they were unfit to fight.

Even then they did all they could to find a way to contribute. My dad presented himself for service but was medically disqualified. He moved to Arizona just so he could work as a volunteer who hand-cranked propellers to start engines at an airfield.

What a contrast to the national conditions just twenty-five years later. American soldiers were again needed for the battlefield. But this time the war was not as popular. Almost no one volunteered for Vietnam. Most of those who fought had to be compelled into service through a military draft. And not a few of those who were conscripted went to college or even left the country in order to defer or dodge the draft.

When it comes to serving in the local church, most professing Christians seem to follow either the World War II model or the Vietnam model. Some are eager to serve. Regardless of their age, and even though it may involve great personal cost, they will volunteer because their heart compels them to do something for the work of God in the church. But many others appear to do all they can to avoid serving. They don't come looking for ways to serve; leaders have to go to them and draft them. When they do serve, they do so reluctantly. They accept a ministry only out of a sense of sheer obligation, and they count the days until their hitch is up.

Which of these two kinds of "servants" is more like Jesus?

Which brings more glory to God?

Which has more love for God?

Which demonstrates more knowledge of God?

Which enjoys God and the people of God more and brings more pleasure to the heart of God?

Which sounds more like you?

Let's look at some reasons that, if you are a Christian, you should serve in the church.

SERVICE MAKES US MORE LIKE JESUS

Remember what Jesus said of Himself: "For even the Son of Man did not come to be served, but to serve, and to give His life a ransom for many" (Mark 10:45). On the night before He was crucified, He served His disciples by washing their feet and said, "Yet I am among you as the One who serves" (Luke 22:27). This deed was no novelty; it characterized His life. Although Jesus was God, He was also the humblest, most servant-hearted man who ever lived. And never did He demonstrate His willingness to do the lowliest form of service more than when He was with the people of God. As Jesus served the Father by serving the Father's children, so should we.

Jesus did not come only to forgive our sin, but also to make us holy—that is, to make us like Himself. He did not live and die for us that we would be forgiven and yet unchanged. The plan of God, predestined before the foundation of the world, is for His people "to be conformed to the image of His Son" (Romans 8:29). And the Son characterized Himself as the "One who serves."

Does it matter to you how much you are like Jesus? Do you ever wonder how you can become more like Jesus? One thing you can do is serve as Jesus served. The work of the church is the work of God on the earth. If Jesus were in your church, can you imagine that He would do nothing? Would He simply attend the worship service, perhaps give a little on occasion, and then leave? Do you think He would serve or merely observe? You know the answer.

SERVICE BRINGS GLORY TO GOD

If you are a Christian, God has given at least one spiritual gift to you. In 1 Peter 4:10–11, God's spiritual gifts are divided into two general categories—speaking gifts and serving gifts. That is, some of us are gifted in areas that emphasize speaking for God, while others of us are blessed with gifts oriented more toward activity for God. (Note that those with speaking gifts are not excused from practical service, and those with action-oriented gifts are not exempted from witnessing and teaching.)

Whatever your gift, God gave it to you for you to use in His service. And the result of serving Him with your gift is glory to God. Follow Peter's thought carefully: "As each one has received a special gift, employ it in *serving one another* as good stewards of the manifold grace of God. Whoever speaks is to speak, as it were, the utterances of God; whoever serves is to do so as one who is serving by the strength which God supplies; *so that* in all things *God may be glorified* through Jesus Christ, to whom belongs the glory and dominion forever and ever. Amen" (1 Peter 4:10–11 NASB, italics added).

Notice that Peter, who was writing to Christians, spoke of serving *one another*. Taken in context we learn that using our spiritual gifts to serve in and through the church is one of the ways we bring glory to God. Any service for God in His church—teaching, committee work, elder or deacon ministry, nursery service, showing mercy, serving food, music ministry, taking care of the facilities—brings glory to God.

On the other hand, a professing Christian who fails to serve in the church of Jesus Christ fails to give glory to God in a very noticeable way.

Serving God in His church says to others that you love Him and that He is *worthy* of serving. It says that you believe God is so great and the work of His kingdom so important that the costs of laying down your life to serve Him are not too much. This glorifies God before the Christian and the non-Christian, to those inside and those outside the church who see you serving. But when you don't serve God, that says God is not worth serving, and that diminishes His glory before others.

In high school and college I worked for my dad at the small town radio station he managed. Not only did I love him, but I cared about his reputation—his "glory"—before others. I knew that the quality of my work would reflect on him, not only before my fellow employees, but to the people throughout the listening area as well. If I were lazy, I knew that others who worked at the station would have reason to think less of my dad. If I did a poor job on the air, I could imagine people throughout the county thinking he hired me only because I was his son, not because I was qualified. And it grieved me whenever another announcer or staffer worked carelessly. I didn't want anyone to disregard my father because of how others and I worked for him.

The same is true in the family of God. When a person will not serve God within the local church—which is the main way God has chosen to do His work on the earth—what does that say to others about that person's God? Who would be attracted to a God who evokes no more devotion than that?

We should serve God not just because it is a duty, because serving Him is much more than that. We should serve God because it glorifies God. He is worthy of everything we can do for Him and His church. Wouldn't you agree?

SERVICE DEMONSTRATES A KNOWLEDGE OF GOD

Serving God in His church is an indication that you have received His grace. Working in the church is not an infallible indication of salvation, of course. Some people mistakenly think they are right with God just because they serve in their local church. That's a terrible misunderstanding of the gospel that says that we are saved by God's grace through faith in Jesus Christ without any contribution from our good works (Ephesians 2:8–9; Titus 3:5–6). Serving God doesn't mean you are His child any more than working for anyone else makes you his or her child.

Moreover, just because a person serves in the church doesn't mean he or she serves *God.* But the person who *has* turned to God *will* demonstrate it by serving Him. Broadly speaking then, believers in Christ are characterized by serving in His church and unbelievers are not. You may even see the unconverted *attending* church on bright Sunday mornings, but it's unlikely that you'll notice them consistently working in a local church.

Service to God has always shown generally who is right with God and who is not. Four hundred years before Christ, the prophet Malachi wrote, "Then you shall again discern between the righteous and the wicked, between one who serves God and one who does not serve Him" (Malachi 3:18). Who is righteous? The "one who serves God." Who is wicked? The "one who does not serve Him." Those who are content not to serve in the work of God are those who do not know God. But those who do know Him can't help serving Him. They cannot be content for very long to ride the bench in the kingdom of God.

Another noteworthy Scripture here is Ephesians 2:10: "For we are His workmanship, *created in Christ Jesus for good works,* which God prepared beforehand that we should walk in them" (italics added). Those who are "created in Christ Jesus," that is, those who are true Christians, were created "*for* good works." Not only that, "God prepared beforehand that we should walk in them."

How then will a person who genuinely knows God through Christ live a lifetime and *not* do what God created him to do and *not* do what God prepared him to do before the foundation of the world? And how can a person sincerely believe that he can do the good works God has created him to do without doing many of them in and through the one organization Christ built for expressing His work in the world?

Listen to the apostle Paul's words to Christians in Philippians 2:13: "For it is God who works in you both to will and to do for His good pleasure." The result of God working His grace into you is the desire and the power to do "His good pleasure." When God has been at work in you, you want to work for God. Once you know Him, you have a compulsion, a feeling that you *have* to do something for Him. Unconverted people just don't think and act this way.

Someone may object, "There are many ways to serve God. All service to God isn't done in the local church."

That's true. In fact, there is a sense in which everything you do every day of your life should be seen as service to God. But serving God with others of His people in the local church is one of the most important ways. And to neglect it, or to seek to minimize your involvement with the body of Christ, or to try to just get by with as little as possible in terms of your service in God's church is not the way the Bible describes authentic Christians.

SERVICE EXPRESSES LOVE FOR GOD

Serving in the church of God is one of the clearest manifestations of loving God Himself. The writer of Hebrews reminded his readers that God would never forget the love they showed to *Him* by ministering to His *people*: "For God is not unjust to forget your work and labor of love which you have shown toward His name, in that you have ministered to the saints, and do minister" (Hebrews 6:10). The people of God show their love for God by serving the church of God.

Obviously, the church is not the only place to serve God. We serve Him in private expressions of our love. Luke 2:37 says that Anna "served God with fastings and prayers night and day." You serve God when you do your job as unto Him (Colossians 3:23–24). You serve Him when you give a cup of cold water in His name. According to Matthew 25:40, Jesus will say at the Judgment regarding how we've ministered to others through providing nourishment or clothing or visitation, "Assuredly, I say to you, inasmuch as you did it to one of the least of these My brethren, you did it to Me."

But serving Him through serving in His church is another unconcealed way the Lord wants us to express our love for Him. Consider the implications of Galatians 6:10, "Therefore, as we have opportunity, let us do good to all, *especially* to those who are of the household of faith" (italics added). If when we "do good to all" we are doing good to Christ, then if we love Christ we should especially do good to the household of faith, for that says to Him, "I love You." And what better way is there to regularly do good to the household of faith than by serving in church ministries to them and with them?

Non-Christians may serve in the church out of a sense of sheer obligation. Christians, on the other hand, perform the duty of service because of their deep love for the One they serve. Serving God becomes like the labor of the Jewish patriarch Jacob who worked in the flocks of his future father-in-law as a bridal price for the one he loved: "So Jacob served seven years for Rachel, and they seemed only a few days to him because of the love he had for her" (Genesis 29:20). Has love for God ever caused you to feel that way in the service of God? I have served in church ministries that would be prison-like drudgery to those who don't love God, and yet I found deep, inexplicable fulfillment in them.

A missionary in Africa was asked if he really liked what he was doing. His response was unexpected. "Do I like this work?" he said. "No. My wife and I do not like dirt. We have reasonably refined sensibilities. We do not like crawling into vile huts through goat refuse. . . . But is a man to do nothing for Christ he does not like? God pity him, if not. Liking or disliking has nothing to do with it. We have orders to 'Go,' and we go. Love constrains us."[1] Love for God makes a delight out of duty. It lifts even the most mundane ministry—whether overseas missionary work or service in the local church—out of the realm of repetitious responsibility.

Some may try to serve God without loving Him, but no one can love God without serving Him. As Spurgeon boldly declared, "He is no Christian who does not seek to serve His God."[2]

SERVICE BRINGS PLEASURE TO GOD AND PEOPLE

Christians who serve God with the right motives experience what King David exclaimed in Psalm 40:8, "I delight to do Your will, O my God." There is delight in doing what we were created to do (remember Ephesians 2:10). The will of God is that His people serve in His church, and to do this brings them great delight and pleasure.

In the Academy Award winning, true-to-life film *Chariots of Fire,* one of the two main characters is Scotsman Eric Liddell. Liddell was a Christian who ultimately died as a martyred missionary in a Japanese prison camp in China during World War II. But he was also the greatest athlete Scotland had ever produced. As the story develops, Liddell's sister Jenny becomes worried that his training for the Olympics will turn his head from going to the mission field as planned following college graduation. Finally he has to explain to her why he continues to pursue the Olympics (where he eventually won a gold medal) over her protests.

"Jenny, Jenny," says Eric as he grasps her gently by the shoulders, "I believe God made me for a purpose—China. But when He made me, He also made me fast. And when I run, I *feel* His pleasure."

When we serve God in the church, it can be work, sometimes *exhausting* work, just as it was for Eric Liddell to train for and run a 400-meter race. Despite the fatigue, though, when a Christian runs in God's service, he can feel His pleasure. Working in the church is not bare duty to him. There is a delight in his soul that comes from serving his King. He finds pleasure in pleasing God.

Service Gives Pleasure to the One Serving

What if God would not allow you to serve Him? How would you feel? Suppose you were told by those in your church, "Just sit back, relax, and enjoy the ministries of the church. Everything will be done for you."

For a short while, perhaps, it might be enjoyable. But let's imagine that, with a growing restlessness to do something useful for the work of God, you said, "May I help take up the offering today?"

"No thanks," would be the response, "we'll manage just fine."

Later you might offer, "Let me set up for the event tonight."

"No, no," you kept hearing, "don't do a thing. We don't need you. Let us do everything for you."

Could you stand that? That would drive me insane. The pleasure is not in the avoidance of service, but in serving. How could any child of God find pleasure and satisfaction in *not* serving God?

Service Gives Pleasure to Others

When you serve in the church it brings pleasure to the people of God too. In Acts 20:17–38, where the apostle Paul gives his farewell to the elders of the Ephesian church, he recounts how he served them for three years. We're told that when he finished talking "they all wept freely, and fell on Paul's neck and kissed him" (Acts 20:37). Why did they react so? Because his ministry had brought so much pleasure to them. God had blessed them through the words and works of Paul, and they couldn't bear the thought of not seeing him again.

Think of some of the people who have served God greatly. Think of Paul, Martin Luther, John Calvin, Jonathan Edwards, Charles Spurgeon, George Mueller, Hudson Taylor, Jim and Elisabeth Elliot, Corrie ten Boom, Billy Graham. Their service to God has been a delight to countless others.

Let's bring it down a notch in terms of fame and notoriety, but think of others you know who have served God wholeheartedly—a favorite preacher of yours, or a missionary or Christian businessperson you've known. They have served God, and as a result they've blessed others and blessed you.

As these dear brothers and sisters of yours have served God they have blessed your life. That's because serving God brings blessing and pleasure to other people. When you serve in the church it gives you pleasure, but it also gives pleasure to others.

Service Gives Pleasure to God

Additionally, serving in the church brings pleasure to the heart of God. "But do not forget to do good and to share," Hebrews 13:16 reminds us, "for with such sacrifices God is well-pleased."

The last chapter of the Bible gives us a glimpse of eternity in heaven saying, "And there shall be no more curse, but the throne of God and of the Lamb shall be in it, and *His servants shall serve Him*" (Revelation 22:3, italics added). What service does God need rendered in heaven? There are no more people to evangelize, no more needs to meet, no more church buildings to build and maintain. And if there is something to do, why not let the angels do everything? We will serve because it brings pleasure to the heart of God for us to serve Him. It will bring Him (and us!) pleasure then when we serve in His city, and it brings Him pleasure now when we serve in His church.

HOW IS YOUR SERVICE QUOTIENT?

Is your church stronger because of you?

Nutritionists speak of "empty calories." In order for these calories to be processed the body must use some of its nutritional resources, yet empty calories do little or nothing to nourish the body in return. Calories from other types of food, however, not only take from the body's strength as they are metabolized, they replenish it.

Do you receive more ministry from the church than you minister to it? God intends for every member of the church body to be served by it, and there are times when even the most spiritually mature members will receive more ministry than they give. Nevertheless, the goal for each of us should be to serve in the church in such a way that it is stronger because we are there.

Everyone who really wants to can do something to strengthen the work of the church. I've visited many homebound or nursing home Christians who maintained a ministry even though they could never attend the church. They prayed faithfully, some even as a part of the church's prayer ministry. Some had a ministry of encouragement through cards or calls; still others determined to be an encourager to all who visited them. Regardless of your limitations of time, strength, or money, your church should be stronger because of you.

Do you do a servant's work with a servant's heart?

The reason some are unwilling to serve or unwilling to serve very long is that they don't have servants' hearts. They do the work of a servant on the outside but they don't have servants' hearts. Then when they are treated like servants—which inevitably happens to those who serve—they quit.

Until you realize that every follower of *the* Servant is also called to be a servant, you'll have difficulty serving, no matter where you try to serve in the church. Every ministry becomes mundane at times. Every ministry is underappreciated. Every ministry feels the sharp sting of criticism sooner or later. Every ministry sometimes seems barren of God's blessing. And unless in these times you can fall back upon the call of God to be a servant, you will become disillusioned and eventually walk away from every place of service you ever fill.

There are moments when I, too, want to walk away from the

ministry. That happens to everyone who serves in the church, whether vocationally or as a volunteer. A pastor friend with a much-admired ministry called this week and as he told me his frustrations said, "Sometimes I wonder what it would be like just to move to a rural town and open a feed store." I've felt exactly as he did that day. But no matter how low my strength for service sinks, there is always this concrete foundation: God has called me. Despite the discouragement I may feel at a given moment, I know there is no happiness in *not* serving Him. Remembering my call—that I am the Servant's servant—helps me maintain a servant's heart and stay faithful to my ministry in the church.

Are you a consistent worker, not a convenience worker?

Too many people have decided that they will serve in the church only occasionally and when it's convenient. They are convenience workers rather than consistent workers. The church needs servants: people who will make long-term commitments and be dependable. The classic example is a Sunday school or Bible study teacher. She or he prepares faithfully every week and serves God and His church loyally and steadfastly. Of course, many other ministries require the same regular commitment. No church can be effective without people like this.

However, there is a lack of commitment in the church. Fewer people want to commit to an ongoing ministry. More and more leaders hear, "I'll help out when I can," and, "Call on me when you really need me." The most important ministries of a church cannot function well with that level of involvement. The church needs soldiers who will enlist and fill the ranks, not people who will help only as last-minute reinforcements and if the battle won't last too long.

To quote Spurgeon again, "We want labourers, not loiterers. We need men on fire, and I beseech you ask God to send them. The harvest can never be reaped by men who will not labour."[3]

The apostle Paul realized that it was consistent ministry *through* hardship that demonstrated that he was a true servant of God: "But in all things we commend ourselves as ministers of God: in much patience, in tribulations, in needs, in distresses, in stripes, in imprisonments, in tumults, in labors, in sleeplessness, in fastings" (2 Corinthians 6:4–5). Observe that it was *in* these things that he proved himself to be a minister of God. This litany of difficulties means that it was never convenient for Paul to serve. But his service was consistent regardless of the hardships—and that was one indication that he really was a servant of God. Dedicated workers are the kinds of servants the church needs today.

Will you resolve never to retire from serving in the church?

Paul warned his readers in 2 Thessalonians 3:13, "But as for you, brethren, do not grow weary in doing good." Why does he warn of this? Because it happens to all of us. Everyone tires of his place of service sometime. When year follows year, and weariness follows sameness, some are ready to say, "I don't want to keep on."

One pastor/author wrote of a woman who worked in the nursery of the church for six years. Then she "retired." Perhaps she did need a break, but she saw it as a permanent change. In a few months, though, she volunteered for regular nursery duty again.

"I went to the adult class and received some wonderful teaching," she explained. "Then I went to the morning worship service and received more wonderful teaching. The same is true for the evening service and the Wednesday night Bible study. Finally it hit me that at most services, all I did was receive. The nursery program was the one main place in the church that I gave!"[4]

Contrast her story with that of an older couple, on whose shoulders many ministries of the church had been carried for many years, who once told me, "We've served our time; now we're going to leave it to the younger ones." And they dropped out of service to the church completely.

Don't quit serving when you are most qualified to serve. Don't lay aside your experience when it is most valuable. Don't look for a rocking chair in the church. Die in the harness, if you are able, not out in the pasture.

Are you serving faithfully in the church?

In Mark 14 a woman anointed the feet of Jesus with a costly perfume valued at a year's wages. When His disciples began to complain about how the perfume could have been put to better use by selling it for the poor, Jesus rebuked them and said, "She has done what she could" (Mark 14:8). She had many limitations in what she could do for

Jesus, but she did what she could to serve Him. Have you done what you could? Are you doing what you can?

Our attitude should never be, "How little can I serve in the church without my conscience bothering me?" but "How *much* can I serve without neglecting my other God-given priorities?" That's the right attitude of the one who has turned from living for himself to serve the living God.

In the definitive best-seller on Pearl Harbor—*At Dawn We Slept*—Gordon Prange closes with these words:

> Of infinitely more value than the repair of shattered ships was the welding together of the American people into a mighty spear and shield of determination. No more did Americans ask whose fight it was or question what they should do about it. . . . The Japanese gave each American a personal stake in the titanic struggle for the minds and bodies of mankind which raged in Europe and Asia. After December 7, 1941 Americans no longer could look upon the war from a distance as an impersonal, ideological conflict. The sense of outrage triggered a feeling of direct involvement which resulted in an explosion of national energy. The Japanese gave the average American a cause he could understand and believe to be worth fighting for.[5]

After the crucifixion and resurrection of Jesus Christ, and after your salvation, Christian, you should not have to ask whose fight the church is in and what you should do about it. These things give you a personal stake in the kingdom of God and its quest for the souls of mankind. No longer can you look upon the war from a distance. Love for God should give you a feeling of direct involvement in the work of God and cause an explosion of supernatural energy for that work. He has given you a cause that you can understand and in which you can have the honor to serve.

CHAPTER EIGHT

WHY GIVE TO THE CHURCH?

. . . . ✤ . . . .

It is by divine design that local churches
provide the primary context in which
Christians are to use their material possessions
to further the work of God's kingdom.

Gene Getz

All churches talk about is money!"

That's what Kathy's neighbor told her when she rejected an invitation to church.

Kathy herself said that she grew up in a church where it seemed that giving was stressed every Sunday. Endless appeals for money were made, usually for the debt on a new building or to prop up an old one. And they were given with more pleading, passion, and enthusiasm, remembers Kathy, than the sermons, prayers, or anything else. So the general impression conveyed was that nothing else mattered as much as money.

There's no denying that some churches—just as some media ministries—present themselves as little more than perpetual fund-raising machines. But it doesn't take much experience in churches to know that, in all denominations, such churches are the exception, not the rule. Few of even the most faithful church attenders can endure for very long a church that's always goading for giving.

Nevertheless, the standard stereotype among non-attenders is that all preachers are little more than money-mad, religious racketeers, and that they see every church service as an opportunity to harangue about money and to call for your cash in the name of God.

In light of this common misconception, why bring up the subject? Why reinforce the prejudice by writing on giving to the church?

The issue of giving to the church should be raised occasionally because of the *biblical reasons* that Christians should give to their local church.

GIVING SHOWS LOVE AND GRATITUDE FOR JESUS CHRIST

If you are a Christian, the main reason you should give to the church is that you love Jesus Christ and are grateful for what He has done for you.

This was the motivation from which Paul wanted the Corinthian Christians to give. As an apostle, he had the authority to command them to give, but he didn't exercise that authority. These believers had voluntarily promised to give an offering that Paul could take to the poverty-stricken Christians in Jerusalem, but they hadn't followed through on their commitment.

Some churches in Macedonia that were much poorer than the Corinthians had already given far beyond their means (cf. 2 Corinthians 8:1–4). In 2 Corinthians 8:8–9 Paul asks the Corinthian church to examine their love for Christ by comparing their default with what the Macedonians had done and with what Christ has done for them. "I speak not by commandment," the apostle said, "but I am testing the sincerity of your love by the diligence of others. For you know the grace of our Lord Jesus Christ, that though He was rich, yet for your sakes He became poor, that you through His poverty might become rich."

Note that Paul was testing the "sincerity of [their] love" by their *giving*. Love for Christ, above all else, was to be the reason they brought their coins to church for this offering. But note also that he reminds them of how Jesus, though He was rich, impoverished Himself by coming to earth in order to enrich them with the blessings of eternal life and eternal heaven. In short, apart from their love for Him, they should also give out of thankful hearts for the wealth Christ had given them.

Of course, God has inspired and preserved Paul's words, not only for those Corinthian Christians of two thousand years ago, but for us as well. Despite all the differences in time and culture between us and those believers, the motivation for giving should be the same for us as it was for them. We, too, should give because of our love for Jesus Christ and because of our gratitude for His giving us immeasurable riches we never could have acquired on our own.

In the next chapter of this letter to the Corinthians, Paul gives further instructions about giving: "So let each one give as he purposes in his heart, not grudgingly or of necessity; for God loves a cheerful giver" (2 Corinthians 9:7). I could say much more about this verse, but I'll simply point out this for now: Giving should come from the *heart*. All true love gives, and love for God is no exception. The hand that gives to God should merely be an extension of a heart that loves God. You should give to the church because you love the Head of the church, Jesus Christ.

Yesterday I got behind a car with a license plate that read "Disabled Veteran." That identification allows the driver certain privileges because of what he suffered on behalf of others. Imagine a government official who resents those privileges and who foolishly proposes a law that revokes them. Long lines of opposition would argue, "These disabled veterans are people *we asked* to go and fight for us. They went willingly and sacrificed a great deal on our behalf. Because of what they did for *us then,* it is *our* responsibility to give on *their* behalf *now.* And realizing what they did for us, if you don't have any affection for them, something is wrong."

We should give to Christ through His church for the same reasons. Remembering what He has done for us—what and where we would be without Him, what He has waiting for us, etc.—should crack the crust that tends to form over our feelings of love and gratitude for Christ. "Though He was rich, yet for your sakes He became poor, that you through His poverty might become rich" (2 Corinthians 8:9). Think of that, and nothing else, for a mere two minutes and I'm confident that, if you are a Christian, the Holy Spirit will help you overcome any reluctance to give to Jesus' church.

THE CHURCH IS THE ONLY ORGANIZATION JESUS SAID HE WOULD BUILD

In Matthew 16:18 Jesus said to His disciples, "I will build My church." The church (in this case referring to all Christians of all time everywhere) belongs to Him, for when He calls it "My church" He acknowledges His ownership. And not only does the church as a whole belong to Christ, but every local expression of it belongs to Him as well. So when you give to the church you attend, you are giving to what Jesus owns and building what He builds. To think of it another way, you are giving to Jesus to help Him build His church.

It can be a good thing to give to ministries other than the church. But only one organization is the church, the bride of Christ for whom He died. "Christ also loved the church and gave Himself for her" (Ephesians 5:25). All other ministries exist (or should exist) to support the church. That's why the term *parachurch ministry* is applied to such Christian organizations: the prefix *para* means "by the side of." But if our primary giving is to any other ministry than the local church, we are actually helping to displace the church.

Pastor, professor, and author Gene Getz, in *A Biblical Theology of Material Possessions,* writes forcefully about the priority of giving to the church:

> Any view, then, of how Christians should use their material possessions must focus first and foremost on local churches. This is what we see in the Bible. To bypass this important concept in Scripture is, in essence, to ignore what is recorded by gifted men inspired by the Holy Spirit. Furthermore, . . . if Christians bypass the concept of the local church, they will inevitably violate a number of other important supracultural principles. . . . Before we support any particular parachurch ministry financially, it is important to view that ministry through the lens of biblical ecclesiology [i.e., the Bible's teaching on the church]. In other words, we must carefully evaluate the function and goals of every parachurch ministry by what Scripture teaches about the local church.[1]

If you love Jesus, you will want to give to support what He is doing in the world. And what is He doing? He is doing what He said He would do—"I will build My *church*."

GIVING HELPS FULFILL THE GREAT COMMISSION

Before He ascended to heaven, Jesus said, "Go therefore and

make disciples of all the nations, baptizing them in the name of the Father and of the Son and of the Holy Spirit, teaching them to observe all things that I have commanded you; and lo, I am with you always, even to the end of the age" (Matthew 28:19–20).

You can't go to all nations, but others are willing to go on your behalf. You can't be a missionary to all fifty U.S. states, but others are willing to go for you. When you give to your local church, your church takes a portion of your gift and uses it to send and support those who will go to other places and make disciples for Christ.

So even if you aren't happy with everything going on in your church and aren't comfortable about supporting every ministry there, when you give to the church you are also helping many others endorsed by your church that are worthy of your support. You provide resources for men and women who have sacrificed much; left their homes, friends, and extended families; turned their backs on more lucrative opportunities; and walked away from a familiar culture. It may be very hard for them to live where they serve. But by giving to your local church, you are making things easier.

GIVING IS A FORM OF WORSHIP

"Giving is preeminently an act of worship," writes Richard B. Cunningham. "It ought then to be a focal point of thanksgiving and self-dedication in weekly worship."[2]

When the church at Philippi collected money for the furtherance of Paul's ministry, he described their giving as "a sweet-smelling aroma, an acceptable sacrifice, well-pleasing to God" (Philippians 4:18). He says to them in effect, "What you gave to me through your church was, like the placing of a sacrificial lamb on an altar in the Old Testament, an act of worship to God." Paul also teaches them—and us—that God is well-pleased when we worship by giving, just as He is when we worship by praying or singing praise.

Although it's true that giving to the church helps pay the bills of its ministry (a proper motive on which I will elaborate later), it's more important to see the act of putting money in an offering plate as an expression of devotion to God. In fact, we call it an *offering* plate (or bag or box) because it is the receptacle of a gift we *offer* to God, and giving to God *is* worship. It's worship because when you give to God through the church you are giving a part of yourself. You exchange a significant measure of your life and labor for salary or wages, and when you give some of that money to God you give that which represents *you*. (Precisely because a person is giving himself when he gives to the church is why some find it so hard to give.)

So when you give, you might want to utter a brief, silent prayer such as "Thank You, Lord," or "I love You, Lord," or "Father, this represents all of me." Otherwise your *act* of worship may not convey *actual* worship. Just as a preacher can preach without thinking of God, or a church member can sing a hymn without thinking of God, so you can give without thinking of God. This is hypocrisy at worst and spiritual carelessness at best.

One other thought about giving in congregational worship: Giving to the church testifies to the church, to unconverted attenders, and to your family of your love for God. If outsiders happen to notice that some of those who lead in worship, or those who are evidently pillars of the church, don't give, wouldn't they say to themselves, *There must be something very wrong with the church if most people, including the leaders, don't give*? When we do give, we become living testimonies that God is worthy of worship and that His church is worthy of support.

GIVING IS A FORM OF FELLOWSHIP

Giving to the church is not only an expression of worship to God, but also of fellowship with His people. In the church, shared giving is a part of shared life.

No church modeled this better than that church full of new Christians in the beginning of the book of Acts. They proved that their heart and soul were in their new community by their giving to the community: "Now the multitude of those who believed were of one heart and one soul; neither did anyone say that any of the things he possessed was his own, but they had all things in common" (Acts 4:32).

The Greek word translated here as *in common* is formed from the same root as *koinonia,* the word for fellowship. Although similar, this word (*koinon*) has more of a financial emphasis to it than *koinonia*. It was used to refer to a joint pool of funds or a shared account. Some who misunderstand life in the early church have thought that this verse speaks of a form of communism. Not so. The attitude in communism is "What's yours is mine," but the attitude of these Christians was "What's mine is yours." They shared materially and financially with the church because they shared a supernatural life with the church.

We ought to be aware of giving to each other when we give to the church. As we give together we provide things such as classrooms, utilities, literature, equipment, and supplies that are used by each other for the work of the church. Our giving enables ministries of the church that strengthen us in return. We *are* the church of Christ, and when we give to the church we are giving to each other as well as to Him.

We ought also to feel a sense of Christian community in giving together to a common cause. By giving to our church we share together in the work of Christ's kingdom. Through giving we unite to shoulder the burden of evangelism and missions, of building up believers, of feeding the hungry, of meeting the practical needs of hurting people. These things are the mutual responsibility of the church body. How could anyone want no part of giving to the church and still feel a part of the church?

My mother is one of four children. In the years before her parents died, there were times when the whole family—the children, their spouses, and the grandchildren—got together to buy a large Christmas gift for my grandparents. If I had never been a part of this family, it never would have crossed my mind to be a part of this combined giving. But since I share a part in the life of this family, I wanted to share in the giving. Giving together was part of what it meant to be a family. The same is true in the family of God. Those who live together should give together.

Giving to the church also strengthens fellowship in the sense that it weakens selfishness. It combats the inborn tendency to want to keep everything for ourselves. After all, there's always a use for the money in the family, the house, at school, or elsewhere besides giving it to the church, isn't there? That's why I have copied from others the helpful habit of giving to the church with the first check written out of each paycheck. I want to give to God first because He is first in my life. Otherwise, if I wait to give out of what's left over, there won't be anything left. The result of that is not only disobedience to God, but an unsettling sense of lack of love for God and of slack in the bonds of fellowship.

GIVING TESTIFIES OF A CHANGED
LIFE AND A CONCERN FOR OTHERS

One of the descriptions of life in the early church is in Acts 4:34–37. In this passage is a remarkable testimony of unselfishness and changed lives:

> Nor was there anyone among them who lacked; for all who were possessors of lands or houses sold them, and brought the proceeds of the things that were sold, and laid them at the apostles' feet; and they distributed to each as anyone had need. And Joses, who was also named Barnabas by the apostles (which is translated Son of Encouragement), a Levite of the country of Cyprus, having land, sold it, and brought the money and laid it at the apostles' feet.

There were at this time thousands of people who had come to Jerusalem because of Pentecost (which occurred in Acts 2), one of the three great annual Jewish religious feasts. These pilgrims had placed their homes and businesses in the care of others and, in some cases, traveled for weeks from regions all around the Mediterranean Sea. When the Spirit of God fell in great power, many of these people were converted.

Large numbers of these new Christians returned home and became the nucleus of the church in their homelands, but some of them said, "I'm not going home. My life is here now." They abandoned their jobs, houses, and possessions for the love and joy of the spiritual home they had found in the Jerusalem church. So the Jerusalem believers found themselves surrounded by Christian brothers and sisters who were suddenly homeless and jobless. In quick response, those such as Barnabas who had houses and lands would sell them as needed and give the money to the church for distribution so that people's needs were met. By doing so they demonstrated that their lives had been changed and that they cared for others. They gave to the church as a testimony that they were not what they used to be and that they felt compassion for those who were in need.

I have a good friend who is in the construction business and is also a skilled handyman at home. He was converted about three years after his wife. During that period he often told her that he never wanted to join a church because he was certain that he would constantly be asked to fix something for the church. Then after he was abruptly and dramatically saved, he began repairing things all over the church building and at the pastor's home *without being asked.* Why? Because Jesus Christ had changed his life and given him a concern for the needs of others, especially those of his Christian family. The same was true of his giving. Even though he has unpleasant childhood memories of being taken to a church where, as he says, every Sunday included a high-pressure appeal for money, after he met Christ he began giving 10 percent and more of his income to his church. A powerful testimony to a transformed life is a transformed checkbook, particularly when those who once decried giving to the church now do it.

GIVING SUPPORTS THE MINISTRY THAT SUPPORTS US

Some people never stop to think how the church pays its bills. Perhaps it never dawns on them that the church has bills. There are churches, mostly very small ones, where the pastor is a volunteer, but in nearly all churches the work of the pastor is honored with a salary. I have never heard of any church getting its water, gas, electricity, or phone service free. And the church orders and pays for its literature just as it buys its office supplies and cleaning products. Where does the money come from for all these things? It should come from those who benefit from the ministry of the church.

I have heard people wonder if it is right for a minister to be paid. Some believe that a minister today should do as the apostle Paul sometimes did; that is, support himself as best he can, then preach and do other pastoral work as time permits.

Financial Support of Ministers Is Biblical

You'll find that the Bible directly addresses this issue in 1 Corinthians 9:6–14. The conclusion in verse 14 is clear: "So also the Lord directed those who proclaim the gospel to get their living from the gospel" (1 Corinthians 9:14 NASB). It is God's plan for those who serve as preachers of the gospel to make their living from this ministry. In new or small ministries where the church is unable to do this, a bivocational ministry is certainly appropriate. But the goal of both the minister and congregation should be for him to have his financial needs met to the point where he can devote all his labors to the work of the church.

Two other passages speak specifically to the responsibility of those who receive from the preacher's ministry:

- Let him who is taught the word share in all good things with him who teaches. (Galatians 6:6)

- Let the elders who rule well be counted worthy of double honor, especially those who labor in the word and doctrine. (1 Timothy 5:17)

In the latter passage it's important to know that in the original language of this verse, the word translated *honor* refers to financial remuneration. With all that could be said about these two verses, what I want to emphasize is simply that the vocational ministers of a church should receive their income from the church.

Financial Support of Ministries Is Practical

How does this happen? Ministers' earnings are disbursed after you voluntarily give to the church. For accountability purposes, in most churches the money is given to the church, not directly to the minister. From the weekly offerings, the church distributes salaries to the pastor and other paid staff members and sends support to missionaries. All the bills and expenses of the church—utilities, literature, maintenance, benevolence, office expenses, etc.—are also met through people's regular gifts to the church.

A good church supports members in incalculable ways. They are taught the Word and way of God. An opportunity is given for the public worship of God, a worship experience far more glorious than an individual could experience alone. Classes for families educate them in the things of God. A banquet of soul-enriching fellowship is always ready for the hungry to take. Loving, practical help arrives in the crises of life. (How doubly difficult it is for those without a church family in times of severe illness, grief, or loss.) From the cradle to the grave, the church is there to support the people of God. And one of the ways to support the ministry that supports you is by giving financially to the church.

To give back to the church is biblical, right, and loving. As one writer reminds us:

> The church is a covenant community, a living organism, where men bind themselves together for internal life, worship, education, service, and proclamation in their own locale and to the ends of the earth. . . . As a member of a covenant community, the Christian commits himself to support the church's internal life and worldwide mission. Thus he will joyfully share in this life and work by giving substantially of his time, talent, and money to his own congregation.[3]

WE SHOULD USE GOD'S MONEY
FOR GOD'S WORK AND GOD'S GLORY

Don't fall for the myth of *my* money. Who owns what you earn, spend, and keep? God does. God owns *you* and everything you call "mine." "The earth is the Lord's, and all it contains," declares Psalm 24:1, "the world, and those who dwell in it" (NASB). The Lord explicitly announces, "For every beast of the forest is Mine, and the cattle on a thousand hills" (Psalm 50:10). Furthermore, " 'The silver is Mine, and the gold is Mine,' says the Lord of hosts" (Haggai 2:8). Our Maker also reminds us that, "Behold, all souls are Mine" (Ezekiel 18:4). And the Scripture affirms, "Whether we live or die, we are the Lord's" (Romans 14:8), and "Do you not know that . . . you are not your own? For you were bought at a price" (1 Corinthians 6:19–20).

One day, of course, God will recall everything. He will gather all souls for judgment and destroy all money, investments, homes, lands, businesses, and possessions (2 Peter 3:10–11). Some day, everything you "own" will not exist, not even as ashes. Your goods are God's. Your money is His. Even though He allows you to earn an income so you can buy the things you need and to provide for your family, it's all *God's* money.

Giving to God's church reminds us that our Creator permanently owns us and all we temporarily have, including our money. This helps us acknowledge that our Provider and Sustainer gives us the jobs by which we earn our money and the health to work in those jobs (Deuteronomy 8:17–18). And since the church is the local expression of God's work, giving to it is the most direct way of using God's money for God's work.

Giving Is a Commanded Privilege

Though a very small boy, I still remember the wide-eyed sense of significance and solemnity I felt about the moment my dad told me he was going to give me an allowance. Fifteen cents per week! My mind raced with excitement about what I would do with my money, but my parents' plan was to teach me from the beginning stewardship of God's money. As a visual aid, they taped three small boxes together. On one they wrote "Church," on the second they marked "Savings," and the third they labeled "Spending." Each week they gave me three nickels, and I was to put one in each box. By this method I learned that all money belongs to God and I recognized the need to give regularly and proportionately to the work of God each Lord's Day.

In 1990 our church was beginning to gather money to build a new worship center. We believed it was God's will for us to attempt to build without debt, although we had no hopes of being able to accomplish this with our own resources. All members were asked to pray about what they should give, to consider selling something of value and donating the proceeds as God directed, or to find other means of greathearted giving.

As pastor, I felt it was my responsibility to be a leader in sacrificially supporting God's work. What kept coming to mind was a collection of two thousand baseball cards from the fifties and sixties. I had bought almost all of them at five cents per pack of five cards, beginning with the days when I had five cents per week to spend. Unlike most of my boyhood pals, for some reason I hadn't thrown away my box of cards when we outgrew the hobby. And despite not thumbing through the cards for years, I kept them after my marriage because I thought they might be a meaningful gift to my own child someday.

The thought of parting with the old box of memories was even sadder than the day I admitted to myself that I'd never be a major league player with my picture on a baseball card. For one thing, it felt almost as though I was selling my childhood. As I flipped through them, card after card summoned up recollections of shade-tree card-trading sessions with buddies; pedaling my bike to a once-thriving small-town downtown to buy a pack; the smell and chalky taste of the flat, pink bubble gum that came in every pack; and sunny, school-free days filled with the crack of a Louisville Slugger™ bat and the smack of a hardball into the palm of an oiled leather glove.

My chin quivered as I turned over the card of my favorite player, Stan Musial. Instantly I was nine years old again and in the backseat of a 1961 Chevrolet in Harrisburg, Arkansas. My family was driving to Little Rock for a state broadcasters' convention my dad would attend. We had stopped for a break and I had asked him for a nickel while the filling station attendant put gas in the car and checked under the hood. I can still see the worn gray boards under my feet as I stepped up onto the wooden sidewalk in front of the dimestore. I bought a pack of baseball cards and hurried back to the car. With the same treasure-hunter's sense of anticipation I had every other time, I carefully unwrapped the colorful waxy paper around the five new cards. There on state highway 14 heading west out of Harrisburg on a summer's day in 1963—Stan's last year in the majors—I first saw my prized Stan Musial card.

Since my dad had now been gone many years, that long-loved piece of cardboard suddenly became the symbol of a precious memory with him that made it more valuable than any collector's purchase offer.

Underneath these feelings lay another emotion that had a depth that took me by surprise. Caffy and I had been unable to have children for thirteen years. As the thought of turning those cards into money came closer to reality, it dawned upon me that I would no longer have them to pass on to my children. Parting with them became, in essence, an acceptance of the fact that I would never be a dad, never have a child to buy baseball cards and memories for, never have a little one to show my Stan Musial card to and tell how I got it.

Giving Brings Rewards

After the man walked out of the house with the box (which itself was given to me by my dad) full of two thousand neatly divided base-ball cards, I sat on our sofa and some of these embedded emotions filled my eyes with tears. Yes, there would be times I would wish I could see and enjoy them again. And some of the cards were quite valuable. I had more than half-a-dozen Mickey Mantles and one rookie card of Nolan Ryan, then some of the hottest cards on the market. I bought the lot for less than $200, and I sold them for several thousand.

But from that moment I have never looked back or regretted selling them. For one thing, I was glad to have a means to give to God's work in a way my heart desired. Second, although I sold the cards I didn't lose the memories. Third, I'm sure this is the kind of giving my father envisioned from me someday when he taught me to give a nickel to God's work before I spent a nickel on baseball cards. Fourth, I believe my heavenly Father smiled. Fifth, I am confident that at the Judgment I will never regret a single nickel I have ever given to the work of God. And sixth, three years after selling the cards (almost to the day) and after sixteen years of being unable to have children, God gave us Laurelen Christiana Whitney, who is worth more than every baseball card in the world. But even if He had not, I have never been sorry about anything I've given for God's work.

GOD PROMISES GENEROUS
BLESSINGS FOR GENEROUS GIVERS

You may be familiar with the passage from Malachi 3:10 where God says,

> "Bring all the tithes into the storehouse, that there may be food in My house, and prove Me now in this," says the Lord of hosts, "if I will not open for you the windows of heaven and pour out for you such blessing that there will not be room enough to receive it."

Regardless of whether you believe that tithing (giving at least 10 percent of your income to God) is only an Old Testament concept or is still expected of God's people today, there is a principle here that is timeless: God gives generously to those who give generously to Him.

A New Testament promise of favor upon those who give unsparingly to the work of God is in 2 Corinthians 9:6–8,

> But this I say: He who sows sparingly will also reap sparingly, and he who sows bountifully will also reap bountifully. So let each one give as he purposes in his heart, not grudgingly or of necessity; for God loves a cheerful giver. And God is able to make all grace abound toward you, that you, always having all

sufficiency in all things, may have an abundance for every good work.

These verses do not teach a prosperity theology, that is, that God wants every Christian to have earthly riches and that giving to God is a Christian's way of getting wealth on earth. Gene Getz points out, "Nowhere in Scripture are Christians taught to *give* in order to *gain* earthly abundance."[4] But a biblical case can be made regarding the generous blessing of God both for our needs in this life and our eternal joy in the next if we are generous and rightly motivated in giving to His work. Reread what the passages *do* say, and remember that these remarkable words are nothing less than the unfailing promise of God Himself. Do you really believe what He says about blessing the person "who sows bountifully"? How could anyone believe these texts and not give generously to God through His church?

MORE APPLICATION ABOUT GIVING

Will you give systematically, proportionately, and sacrificially to your church?

Now that you are, I trust, convinced from Scripture that you should give to the church, let me point out some specifics of *how* to give to your local church.

First, give *systematically*. Systematic giving is taught by Paul in 1 Corinthians 16:1–2: "Now concerning the collection for the saints, as I have given orders to the churches of Galatia, so you must do also: *On the first day of the week* let each one of you lay something aside, storing up as he may prosper, that there be no collections when I come" (italics added). The "first day of the week" was the Lord's Day—Sunday—the day when Christians worship. If possible, I would encourage you to try to give some amount every week. Many people are paid biweekly, monthly, or even receive their income sporadically. Giving on the first day of every week in such cases simply requires dividing your offering and giving part of it each week until you are paid again. Some do this in equal amounts each week; others give most of it on the first Sunday after payday and smaller amounts other weeks.

In any case, use a routine to your advantage. Here are some

ideas: Prepare your gift each Saturday night or Sunday morning as part of your customary preparation for church; if you write checks according to a schedule, make the first check you write be the one to the church; if you give monthly, designate a specific day in every month (such as the first) when you will arrange to give; take your calendar and write giving reminders for the entire year; if you use a computer to organize your finances, set a permanent prompt in your financial software. But however you organize your giving, have a *system*. Make it a simple system, but establish regularity in your giving.

Second, give *proportionately*. Prayerfully set a percentage of your income that you will systematically give to the Lord through your church. Giving that's based upon a predetermined standard helps you avoid questions such as, "Do I have any money left over to give to the church?" or "What do I feel led to give this week?" If you don't give according to a set time and a set amount you'll probably give much less than you think, much less than you could, and much less than you want.

Each believer in the Corinthian church was urged in verse one to give "as he may prosper." So the more you prosper, the higher your rate of giving should be. Sadly, just the opposite is true with most people. Surveys consistently show that the poorest American Christians give the highest percentage of their income to their church, while the wealthiest give the lowest. Still, few in any group seem to give "as [they] may prosper." A study of 100,000 U.S. churches (nearly a third of the country's 350,000 congregations) showed that American church members were giving a *smaller* percentage of their income to the church than they had been twenty-five years earlier (and it was a small percentage then). The average church member in 1993 gave 2.5 percent of his income to God, compared to 3.14 percent in 1968.[5]

As a protection against the temptation to greedily keep more as you make more, and to make sure that you remember to give according to your prosperity, I would encourage you to have an ongoing, lifetime goal of increasing the percentage of your income that you give to God. Even though the percentage increase may only be a tiny one, do your best after every raise, or at the start of each year, to make progress toward this goal.

Third, give *sacrificially*. God inspired the apostle to write, "*Each one* of you lay something aside." That meant that every member of the church, from the wealthiest to the poorest, was to give. Of course, Paul didn't expect each person to give the same amount. What is expected of us is not equal gifts, but equal sacrifice. But rather than wondering if everyone else is sacrificing as much as you, look only at your own giving. And at the risk of sounding redundant, remember that your giving isn't sacrificial unless it's a *sacrifice*. Just because you could use the money on something else doesn't mean you have sacrificed to give. Giving is a sacrifice according to what remains, not what is given.

Giving to the church is of no eternal benefit to you unless you have first given yourself to the Lord.

In 2 Corinthians 8:5, Paul commends the churches of Macedonia. When he describes their giving he says "they first gave themselves to the Lord." They didn't give merely to fulfill some sense of obligation. They willingly gave money because they had already given their lives.

You can't buy God's favor. No amount of money, whether given at one time or over a lifetime, can purchase a ticket to heaven. Until a person comes to Christ—whose death bought pardon for sins—giving to the church brings no gain at the Judgment or beyond. And after a person has turned from living for himself and given his life to Jesus Christ, he must not partition giving from Christian living. "We are well trained," observed Princeton University sociologist Robert Wuthnow, "at putting our faith in one mental box and our finances in another."[6] Instead the follower of Jesus must put himself—his rights, his time, his preferences, his choices, his all—in the offering plate, and not his money alone.

"That's where it all begins," says John MacArthur. "Give yourself to the Lord first, or else the rest is somewhat meaningless."[7]

Have you given yourself to the Lord? If so, do you give to His church like one who is His?

CHAPTER NINE

WHY ATTEND THE ORDINANCES OF THE CHURCH?

. . . . ⚜ . . . .

Ordinances are the [presence of] heaven on earth.
Christ delights to be there with his people.

Thomas Boston

In church one Sunday morning the pastor announces that in the evening a person you do not know will be baptized. Will that information have any measurable impact on your plans for the evening? If you had already decided to attend the ministry of your church that night, would that baptismal announcement add incentive to your decision? Is it possible that the news would influence you to go if you had previously determined to stay at home?

Or perhaps you learn that in an upcoming service the Lord's Supper will be served. Does that fact alone make any difference in how you rate the importance of being at that service? Would you ever change your schedule and your priorities in order to be present at a worship service because the Lord's Supper is to be served there?

For people who claim to be Christians, attending the worship of God with the people of God should *always* be a priority (Hebrews 10:25). But knowing that one of the ordinances of the church will be observed should only add to your determination to be there.

WHAT ARE THE ORDINANCES?

A Christian ordinance is a ceremony that the Lord Jesus Christ has commanded to be permanently practiced by the church. In the

New Testament we find two ordinances given to the church, baptism and the Lord's Supper. Let me reemphasize that these practices are ordained by Jesus Himself—not by tradition, church councils, influential leaders in the history of the church, or even by the apostles.

The ordinances are distinct ceremonies, not just general actions or attitudes. So although love, for example, is commanded by Jesus to be a distinguishing mark for all Christians, love is not an ordinance.

They are also ceremonies that were practiced by churches in the New Testament. That is why most churches today do not consider foot-washing to be an ordinance, even though Jesus washed the apostles' feet and said, "You also ought to wash one another's feet" (John 13:14). Since we do not read of this being repeated regularly as a specific practice by New Testament churches, we believe the apostles understood it to be a living example of the humble, loving service Christians should give to others.

Next, ordinances are practices that should be observed by the church, everywhere she exists, until the Lord Jesus returns. They are permanent and transcultural. There may be many differences, for example, between the life and traditions of the church in suburban America and the church in tribal Africa, but Jesus has ordained that the church in both places baptize believers and observe the Lord's Supper.

Additionally, ordinances are ceremonies given by Christ to the *church,* and not to *individual* Christians. That's why we don't encourage people to baptize their children in the bathtub, for instance, or their newly converted neighbors in the swimming pool at home. That's also why we should not take the Lord's Supper in small groups apart from the rest of the church without the church's blessing.

Only baptism and the Lord's Supper qualify as ordinances of the church. Because of their God-given uniqueness and significance, attendance at these ordinances by those who are Christians is indispensable. "I believe so strongly in a Christian's obedience to those two practices," says John MacArthur, "that I think a Christian should question his own commitment to Christ if he does not observe them."[1]

WHY ATTEND THE ORDINANCE OF BAPTISM?

Jesus teaches that all His followers should be baptized (Matthew

28:19–20). In this chapter, however, the assumption is that you are a Christian and have already identified yourself publicly with Jesus through New Testament baptism (as presented in chapter 2).

The question to be answered here is why, as a Christian, you should always *attend* the public services of your church when others are baptized, even if that baptism involves someone you haven't met.

You Demonstrate Commitment to the Great Commission

In the famous words of Jesus often referred to as the Great Commission, He said, "Go therefore and make disciples of all the nations, baptizing them in the name of the Father and of the Son and of the Holy Spirit" (Matthew 28:19).

Here in the final earthly instructions of Jesus Christ is the command that those who become His disciples should openly identify themselves with Him in a specific way. The sign Jesus chose as the initiatory mark of Christian discipleship is baptism "in the name of the Father and of the Son and of the Holy Spirit."

Every church member would at least give lip service to supporting the Great Commission. We want to reach people for Christ and have them boldly proclaim by their baptism that they have given their lives to Him and His service. Does a person really care about the Great Commission, however, if he doesn't even care enough to come and watch it be fulfilled? It's one thing when a person won't *work* for the Great Commission to happen, but it's another thing when he won't even come to *watch* it happen. You can talk about it, learn about it, even give to it, but are you really concerned about the Great Commission if you will not come with your own church family to a place that's convenient to observe it taking place?

If you are committed to the Great Commission of Christ to "make disciples of all the nations" and to baptize them, you'll prove it by your presence when it happens.

You Show Commitment to the Importance of Baptism

In addition to the Great Commission, many other passages in the New Testament teach the importance of baptism. In Acts 2:38, after Peter had preached to a crowd in Jerusalem about their need for Christ and they had asked what they must do, he said, "Repent, and let every one of you be baptized in the name of Jesus Christ for the remission of sins; and you shall receive the gift of the Holy Spirit."

Although the Bible never makes baptism a condition of salvation, it does closely associate the two. Not only is baptism a public identification of the believer with Christ, it symbolizes much that happens in salvation. It is a picture of the cleansing of the believer's guilt of sin that Christ's death has accomplished. Baptism represents the death of the person without Christ and the raising of the person to a new life with Christ. It also symbolizes the spiritual union of the Christian with Jesus in His death, burial, and resurrection.

Christian baptism is filled with meaning. And the Bible commands us to be baptized when we are born again by the Spirit of God. So when a new believer is baptized, our presence expresses our commitment to the importance of that ordinance.

Do you think baptism is important? Do you think that when a person becomes a Christian he or she should be baptized? If someone in your family were converted, do you think he or she should be baptized? Of course you do, because you believe baptism is a biblical command. If you believe baptism is important, you'll be there when it happens.

You Accept a New Member into the Family

Baptism is an outward, visible symbol of things that have already happened inwardly. When God brings a person into spiritual life, that person enters into the spiritual and invisible body of Christ—the universal church. When that spiritual experience is pictured in water baptism, that is the individual's symbolic entry into the tangible and visible body of Christ—the local church.

How are we to respond when another child of God officially becomes a member of our local expression of God's family? Romans 15:7 says, "Therefore receive one another, just as Christ also received us, to the glory of God." One of the first ways we can show our acceptance of new members of the family is to be there when they formally enter the family, that is, at their baptism.

Your attendance at a person's baptism says that you affirm his obedience to God and the Bible. It expresses your joy in the work of God in his life. It tells him that you care about him.

What if you married and became a new member of a family, but many of your new family members didn't come to the wedding? It might be understandable if they lived far away, but would you feel accepted by them if they were only a few minutes away? Wouldn't it trouble you if they didn't come and welcome you into the family because they said they didn't know you very well, or because they were tired or busy or were leaving town the next day?

What would you think if your family had a new baby born into it, and everyone related to you lived close by, but many of them had no interest in coming to the hospital or no interest in seeing the baby? Would you feel loved and accepted? No, you'd feel unloved and rejected by the family.

That's the same way new Christians might feel when members of their church family won't attend their baptism. By coming we say, "We love you, and we gladly accept you into the family of God in this place."

WHY ATTEND THE ORDINANCE OF THE LORD'S SUPPER?

Whereas baptism is the initial ordinance of the Christian life, the Lord's Supper is the ongoing one. Scriptural baptism occurs only once. Taking the Lord's Supper, however, is an experience that should occur many times each year throughout a Christian's life. And while baptism is something we undergo only once and then *watch* thereafter, the Lord's Supper is an ordinance where attendance should always mean *participation*.

Why is it, then, that Christians should make an extra effort to attend and participate in the Lord's Supper whenever it is offered in their particular church?

It Is Commanded By Jesus

Earlier I noted that the ordinances are not the inventions of men but the instructions of God. The Lord Jesus made a perpetual priority of the Lord's Supper when, in Luke 22:19, "He took bread, gave thanks and broke it, and gave it to them, saying, 'This is My body which is given for you; *do this* in remembrance of Me'" (italics added).

The apostles were the ones who personally received this bread and command from Jesus. But they understood that He did not mean this practice of remembrance for themselves alone, for they in turn established the Lord's Supper in the churches that they founded (1 Corinthians 11:23–26). Jesus' words about the Supper—"do this in remembrance of Me"—are as much for you as for any Christian who ever lived. Will you receive His words? Will you receive His Supper when His church offers it on His behalf?

It Is Loved By Jesus

Jesus inaugurated the Lord's Supper during the final Passover meal He ate with His disciples. Hear His heart, and listen to the emotion put into His words to them in Luke 22:15, "With *fervent desire* I have *desired* to eat this Passover with you before I suffer" (italics added). He anticipated eating "*this* Passover" with them so intensely because it signified so much. It meant that He was nearing the fulfillment of the great mission that had cost Him thirty-three years away from heaven.

The supper also symbolized all He was about to accomplish for His people on the Cross. In short, it represented everything about His life and death to save people of every tongue, tribe, nation, and people. No wonder taking this meal with His disciples meant so much to Him. Do you love what Jesus loves?

It Is Spiritual Participation in the Body and Blood of Jesus

Mysterious, yet real, is the communion that believers have with Christ in the Lord's Supper. "The cup of blessing which we bless, is it not the *communion of the blood of Christ?*" asks Paul in 1 Corinthians 10:16 (italics added). And again, "The bread which we break, is it not the *communion of the body of Christ?*" The word "communion" used twice here is the translation of the word *koinonia* in the original Greek version Paul wrote. In most places in the New Testament the word is rendered "fellowship" (as in Acts 2:42). The verse is saying that when we (i.e., we who already know Christ) take the Lord's Supper cup, we have intimate fellowship with the blood of Christ, and when we eat the bread we share in the body of Christ.

Although He is present everywhere, there is a special presence of Christ at His table. "When we participate in the observance of the Supper we enter into a special communion ["fellowship, participation" from *koinonia*] with Christ," writes New Testament scholar David Dockery.[2]

How far can we go in describing this fellowship? Even the great theologian John Calvin abandoned hope of explaining the relationship between Jesus and a believer during the Lord's Supper: "It is a mystery of Christ's secret union with the devout which is by nature incomprehensible. If anybody should ask me how this communion takes place, I am not ashamed to confess that that is a secret too lofty for either my mind to comprehend or my words to declare."[3] Good Christians differ over the *nature* of this singular intimacy with their Lord, yet when they come believingly to the table there is a sense in which they meet Jesus Himself.

Participation in the Lord's Supper allows us an experience with Christ that cannot be enjoyed in any other manner. Neither prayer, the preaching of God's Word, public or private worship, nor any other means of encounter with the Lord can bring us into the presence of Jesus Christ in exactly the same way. God has given to His children several means of communion with His Son, but one is unique to the Lord's Supper. Further, this communion is spiritual—that is, it does not occur merely by eating the bread and drinking from the cup, but by faith. And even though the bread and the cup do not contain the physical body and blood of Jesus, nor are they changed into them, they really do minister Christ to those who believe.

As we'll see next, the meal is a memorial. Jesus said, "This do . . . in remembrance of Me" (1 Corinthians 11:25). But by taking it we do more than remember Christ; we encounter Him. Our mouth takes the food, but it is our soul that is fed. Spiritual nourishment proceeds from the real, if indescribable, presence of Christ at His table to those who come in faith.

It Is a Memorial to Jesus

My *Webster's Encyclopedic Unabridged Dictionary of the English Language* defines a memorial as "something designed to preserve the memory of a person, event, etc." Jesus appointed the Lord's Supper expressly for this purpose. Instructing the Corinthian Christians about the ordinance, Paul describes the scene in the Upper Room, then quotes Jesus: "And when He had given thanks, He broke it and said, 'Take, eat; this is My body which is broken for you; do this in *remembrance* of Me.' In the same manner He also took the cup after supper, saying, 'This cup is the new covenant in My blood. This do, as often as you drink it, in *remembrance* of Me'" (1 Corinthians 11:24–25, italics added). Thus the Lord's Supper remembers both a person ("do this in remembrance of *Me*") and an event, namely the Cross ("this is My body which is broken for you").

In 1991, the church I was pastoring sent Caffy and me to the U.K. in recognition of our tenth anniversary at the church. One of our most interesting tours was at Westminster Abbey, where many of England's national heroes are buried. All around the interior perimeter of the church and in all the alcoves were tombs and monuments of various types. Some were eight feet wide and ten feet high and covered with sculptured images of the hero, plaques depicting his achievements, and other ornaments displaying his fame. Ironically, in some parts of the building there were so many of these memorials and space was at such a premium that they were placed one in front of the other like files in a forgotten cabinet. A few were pushed to the side and almost completely concealed by irregular columns of stacked plastic chairs. Soldiers and statesmen, scientists and scholars—once the best-known men in the kingdom—were now all but forgotten, for even their memorials are obscured.

But even with the best memorials—massive statues in prominent places or national landmarks such as Mount Rushmore or the Washington Monument—the memory of the person or event erodes with the winds of time. Not so with the memorial to Jesus Christ. For one thing, His memorial is not a monument but an *event*. The Lord's Supper is not a marker to be admired but an event to be experienced. Participation, not just observation, makes the Lord's Supper a different kind of memorial. Further, as mentioned above, Jesus Himself is *present* in the memorial, and not just a memory from long ago and far away.

So the Lord's Supper is a memorial of the person and work of Jesus Christ, especially His death on the Cross to bring us to God. But it is a memorial where the person and work of Jesus Christ are not a mere remembrance from the past but a reality in the present.

Accessible by faith, He is there in the verbal and visual proclamation, and so is His power to do what the Supper portrays. To attend this living memorial gives honor to the One it remembers and proclaims.

It Is a Proclamation of the Death of Jesus

That the Lord's Supper is more than just a look at the past is emphasized in the next verse of Paul's words to the Corinthians on the issue: "For as often as you eat this bread and drink this cup, you *pro-*

claim the Lord's death till He comes" (1 Corinthians 11:26, italics added). The bread symbolizes the human body of Jesus Christ and the drink represents His blood. Together they portray the bloody death of Jesus for the forgiveness of sins and the granting of eternal life.

Since the elements of the Lord's Supper represent the death of Jesus, giving attention to them in a public worship service thereby calls attention to, that is, proclaims, the death of Jesus. The bread and cup take the gaze of the congregation and put it on the Cross. So even when the preaching in the church gets away from the gospel, at least the heart of the gospel is proclaimed if the Lord's Supper is served. Thus whenever the food from the Lord's table is set before our eyes, and we breathe its aroma, and its elements are handled with our hands and tasted with our tongue, it serves as a multisensory reminder that Christ's death is central to our faith. And when you take this simple meal in accordance with the guidelines of Scripture you openly testify to your belief that His death is your life.

Do you care to proclaim the death of Christ? "Well," you may say, "I'm not a preacher or an evangelist. In fact, I'm not even confident in sharing the gospel individually. I don't know how to proclaim the death of Christ." One way you can do so is by participating in the Lord's Supper.

It Is an Anticipation of the Second Coming of Jesus

This same verse (1 Corinthians 11:26) not only stresses the past and the present, but the future as well: "For as often as you eat this bread and drink this cup, you proclaim the Lord's death *till He comes*" (italics added). The Lord's Supper is a look backward to the Cross and a reminder of communion with Christ in the present, but it is also an expression of expectation for His earthly return.

This is one of the parallels between the Jewish Passover meal and the Lord's Supper which Jesus instituted at His last Passover. Theologian and Bible commentator Charles Hodge describes the similarity: "As the Passover was a perpetual commemoration of the deliverance out of Egypt, and a prediction of the coming and death of the Lamb of God, . . . so the Lord's supper is at once the commemoration of the death of Christ and a pledge of his coming the second time."[4]

Many churches today offer the Lord's Supper but deny that Jesus will reappear bodily. And yet, according to this verse, receiving the bread and cup of the Lord is specifically intended to identify you as a believer in His promise to come back to the earth (Matthew 24:30; John 14:3, 28). One day, the ordinance reminds us, the invisible presence of Jesus at the table will be replaced by His physical presence on the planet. Do you believe in His Second Coming? Do you want to "proclaim the Lord's death till He comes"? Then express that by accepting the Lord's invitation to His table every time it is set.

CONCLUDING CONSIDERATIONS

Participating in the ordinances does not make you a Christian.

Through repentance and faith, you must know the Jesus Christ symbolized in the ordinances. Hardly any error is more common than thinking that you are a Christian and you will go to heaven because you are baptized and/or take the Lord's Supper. I've known people who wanted to be baptized again and again, or who tried to take the Lord's Supper as often as possible because they were convinced that such efforts would surely win God's favor.

But the Bible says that it is "not by works of righteousness which we have done, but according to His mercy He saved us, through the washing of regeneration and renewing of the Holy Spirit, whom He poured out on us abundantly through Jesus Christ our Savior" (Titus 3:5–6). You could be baptized and take the Lord's Supper (which surely qualify as "works of righteousness") every day for the rest of your life and you would be no more acceptable to God than when you started. We definitely should participate in the ordinances of the church, but the only basis of expecting entrance into heaven is not the merit of doing these good things, but faith in what Jesus has done.

Participating in the ordinances is more important than almost every reason people give for not participating in them.

It's one thing to be absent from a baptismal or communion service because you are ill or otherwise providentially hindered. It's another to miss simply because you aren't in the habit of going at the time of that service (such as in the evening), or for reasons such as you don't know the one(s) being baptized, you want to get ready for travel or work the next day, you want to watch something on television, or you had other plans. At the Judgment these may not sound as reasonable when considered in light of the command of Jesus to "do this in remembrance of Me."

Those who really want to participate in the ordinances will find a way. I know a quadriplegic man who was baptized by immersion. I've served the Lord's Supper to homebound and shut-in church members. Most of the time nothing hinders professing Christians from attending the ordinances except their own heart. Can a friend of Christ, can someone who says they love Him more than anyone or anything, hear these things and then not come to the table of Jesus or to the baptism of a new brother or sister in His family?

Participating in the ordinances is necessary and a blessing.

God does not call us to do anything that is purposeless or meaningless. If He ordains something, such as participation in the Lord's Supper, then it is necessary for us, even if we don't understand why. And we can add that anything He commands us to do is meant to bless us, for God is good and does good (Psalm 119:68). Not all blessings are recognized in this life or spiritual blessings always felt. Can you be persuaded simply by the Word of God alone that you need the ordinances of God? Will you receive the blessing of God that comes through the proper participation in these ordinances?

Having encountered the Scriptures, how will you respond the next time you hear that announcement at church about an upcoming baptismal service or Lord's Supper observance?

CHAPTER TEN

WHY FELLOWSHIP WITH THE CHURCH?

· · · · · · · ❖ · · · · · · ·

As we value the health of our own souls
and of the Christian church, then,
we must learn to prize fellowship.

J. I. Packer

Emotionally healthy people crave community. God made us with that desire, and we seek to satisfy it in societies of all sorts. This universal longing for community is illustrated by a front-page article in the July 11, 1994, edition of *The Wall Street Journal*. In it, Irving Kristol, a fellow at the American Enterprise Institute, spoke of "a shaking of the foundations of the modern world." Kristol sees "a yawning philosophical vacuum in American life, with people urgently trying to fill it in myriad ways." The article notes his observation: "Membership in evangelical religions is growing, even as New Age philosophies proliferate. The environmental movement, the feminist movement, the rise of alternative medicine, the explosion of street gangs—each represents a hunger for something beyond scientific rationalism, beyond material progress." Kristol's explanation for these societal surges is, "People want more. They want community and they want transcendence."

But they aren't finding it. They didn't find it in the technological advances of "scientific rationalism" or the wealth of "material progress." And they won't find it in a philosophy, movement, gang, recovery group, computer network, or any other type of community which they abandon the foundations of the modern world in order to join. Man-made, human-centered associations and brotherhoods merely moisten the parched longing that our Maker means to saturate in another way.

Spiritually healthy people—Christians who live in faithful response to the Word and Spirit of God—have found the community everyone is searching for. They have found it in what the Bible calls *fellowship*. Fellowship is the community for which God customized us.

Curiously, however, some Christians are tempted to think that they can remain spiritually healthy apart from breathing the fresh air of biblical fellowship. There are degrees of this soul-malady, ranging from those who don't go to church at all to those who attend public worship but never seek meaningful, face-to-face interaction with other believers about the things of God.

Similarly afflicted are those believers who acknowledge the value of fellowship but who are convinced that the fellowship they experience with Christians who providentially cross their path outside the context of a local church is sufficient. In other words, they think, *Why fellowship with the church? God will bring other Christians into my life as I need them.*

Certainly we can have some measure of fellowship with all Christians everywhere whenever we meet them. Most believers have testimonies of serendipitous contacts—on an airplane, for example—with someone whom they discover to be Christian. Immediately there is a sense of identification with that brother or sister that is often followed by wonderful fellowship, even though it is only a brief, once-in-a-lifetime encounter. But consistent and life-sustaining fellowship in the New Testament is inseparably joined to intimacy within a believing community. Note the first description of life in the first church: "And they continued steadfastly in the apostles' doctrine and *fellowship,* in the breaking of bread, and in prayers" (Acts 2:42, italics added).

But why should we fellowship with the members of a local church, especially if we're in a church where we live far from other members, we have a constantly hectic schedule, or we have regular contact with believers outside a church setting?

FELLOWSHIP WITH THE CHURCH IS A UNIQUE PRIVILEGE

Let me define fellowship. The English word is a translation of the New Testament (Greek) word *koinonia* (pronounced coy-no-KNEE-ah). In addition to "fellowship," this colorful word is also rendered "participation," "impartation," "partnership," or "communion" and has the sense of to "share in something." At the time the New Testament was written, *koinonia* was used in secular Greek writings to refer to people sharing in business enterprises, legal relations, citizenship, marriage, and especially friendship.

God inspired Christian writers such as the apostle Paul to use *koinonia* as one description of a believer's relationship with Jesus Christ (1 Corinthians 1:9). Fellowship with Christ involves living, suffering, dying, inheriting, and reigning with Him (Romans 6:6, 8; 8:17; 2 Timothy 2:12). Paul wrote of having a share in Christ's sufferings (Philippians 3:10), but also of sharing in His glory (Romans 8:17). Likewise, he talked about a Christian's fellowship with the Holy Spirit (2 Corinthians 13:14; Philippians 2:1) who indwells each believer in Christ.[1]

Let us be clear, then, that the basis for fellowship with other Christians is the fellowship we have with God through Christ. This is the emphasis in 1 John 1:3, "That which we have seen and heard we declare to you, that you also may have fellowship with us; and truly our fellowship is with the Father and with His Son Jesus Christ." The supernatural quality of the relationship Christians have with each other is because of what we share in Christ.

Commenting on this passage, John MacArthur wrote, "Anybody in fellowship with Jesus Christ is also in fellowship with anybody else in fellowship with Jesus Christ. This is our common ground. It is not social, economic, intellectual, cosmetic, or anything else superficial. *Our common ground is that which is pulsing through the life of every Christian—the heartbeat of God.* Our common ground is that we possess a common eternal life and are children in the same family."[2]

The Unique Blessings of Christian Fellowship

It is this vibrant, vigorous word *koinonia* that the Bible uses when it describes the spiritual bond and dynamic between people in the body of Christ. Together we are participants in the life, death, and resurrection of Jesus Christ. We have communion in eternal life. We are partners in the Great Commission and the work of the kingdom of God. We share a common gift—the indwelling presence of the Holy Spirit.

Thus Christian fellowship is unique. No other relationship compares with it—not the bond between parents and their children, not the love between husbands and wives, not the kinship between brothers or sisters, not the closeness between dear friends. These share the best intimacies of earthly life, but even unbelievers experience them.

By now it is obvious that *koinonia* is much more than just attending worship together (though a measure of it does occur there). Christian fellowship also extends far beyond mere *socializing*. Eating coffee and donuts or cookies and ice cream in the "fellowship hall" does not necessarily mean that *koinonia* has occurred. Yet as common as Sunday morning smiles is the confusion between socializing and fellowship. And the inability to recognize the distinction is unhealthy for the soul. As theologian J. I. Packer puts it:

> It is not a good sign when a person sees no difference between
> sucking sweets and eating a square meal. Equally it is not a good
> sign when Christians see no difference between social activities
> in Christian company and what the New Testament calls fellow-
> ship in Christ.[3]

Many Christians never seem to distinguish between socializing and fellowship. Think of two concentric circles. The larger circle is socializing; the inner one is fellowship. This shows how fellowship always takes place within the context of socializing, but also how we can have socializing without fellowship. Socializing is the larger circle because it involves sharing the common things of human, earthly life. All people can do this, whether or not they are Christians. But Christian fellowship, New Testament *koinonia,* involves the sharing of spiritual life.

Please note that I am not arguing against socializing. It is a gift of God. It is part of being human. The church needs socializing, and so does the individual Christian. But in practice the church has often accepted socializing as a substitute for fellowship, almost forfeiting our spiritual birthright as children of God for something far less valuable.

In *Spiritual Disciplines for the Christian Life* I elaborated further on the discounting of fellowship in favor of socializing:

> It looks like this: two or more Christians can sit together for

hours, talking only of the news, weather, and sports while completely ignoring their need to discuss directly spiritual matters.
I'm not saying that every conversation between Christians must
include references to Bible verses, recent answers to prayer, or
insights from today's devotional time. But I've observed that
many otherwise committed Christians are so independent in their
practice of the Spiritual Disciplines that they almost never talk
about such things on a heart level. And without personal interaction about the mutual interests, problems, and aspirations of discipleship, our spiritual lives are impoverished. Then at the end of
the day, having merely socialized, we think we have had fellowship. Only Christians can have the rich banquet of *koinonia*, but
too often we settle for little more than the fast-food kind of socializing which even the world can experience.[4]

Sharing in the life, death, and resurrection of Jesus Christ and in
the indwelling of the Spirit of God gives us more to talk about than the
world dreams of. Why then are Christian gatherings (whether it's two
believers or the whole church) so often characterized by conversations
about everything *except* the things of God and Christian living?

Fellowship can happen simply by two or more believers in Christ
talking with each other from their knowledge of and experience with
God and His Word. It can happen almost anywhere at almost any time.
A type of fellowship occurs when Christians listen together as God is
revealed through His Word preached. *Koinonia* takes place when
believers pray with each other. Fellowship should always grow in the
soil of small group Bible study. It can be experienced while working in
the church with a fellow member, while ministering with another to
someone in need, or during a team effort to explain the gospel to an out-
sider. It should thrive when Christians eat a meal together. Whenever
the children of God share *earthly* life—husbands and wives at home in
the evening, friends riding in the car or shopping at the mall, moms
exercising with each other, businesspeople on the phone together,
neighbors helping neighbors—they can share their *spiritual* life.

The Subject Matter of Christian Fellowship

I saw an outstanding example of the simplicity and beauty of fellowship with the church not long ago while I was in California to

speak at a church over the weekend. On Saturday I was leading a retreat for the men. After the evening session I gathered with the rest in a large room where refreshments were served. Soon I noticed about a dozen men collected into an informal circle discussing something that obviously interested them all. Nonchalantly making my way beside them, I eavesdropped.

"Well," said the first one I heard, "the doctrine of election really opened up to me when I read Romans 9."

They weren't chatting about work or football, but rather the Bible and theology. As I listened further, they talked with each other about family devotions, the value and methods of keeping a journal, the Cross, prayer, and how to take notes during a sermon. They were whites, blacks, and Hispanics; truck drivers, executives, and farm laborers, men who otherwise probably wouldn't even know each other and would have almost nothing in common, but who hold the dearest things in life together because of their common fellowship with Jesus Christ. And they conversed about spiritual matters as naturally as they would about their children or their lawns.

This *koinonia* is a wonderful privilege. As Scottish pastor and writer Maurice Roberts notes,

> Fellowship between Christians is the gift of God. It is a true means of grace. Christians are spiritual people and they feel comparatively isolated in this world. But God gives them this compensation, that the fellowship they enjoy with like-minded brethren and sisters is marvelously therapeutic and sweet.[5]

God intends for every Christian to enjoy the therapeutic sweetness of fellowship. And the reservoir God made where we may drink these refreshing waters is the local church.

FELLOWSHIP WITH THE CHURCH PROVIDES UNIQUE BENEFITS

Here are some of the ways God blesses His people through the experience of *koinonia* with the church:

You Experience the Grace of God in Ways You Otherwise Cannot

As previously noted, after Pentecost, the members of the church in Jerusalem "continued steadfastly in the apostles' doctrine and *fellowship,* in the breaking of bread, and in prayers" (Acts 2:42, italics added). They found something in fellowship that they couldn't experience in listening to the apostles teach, or in eating and taking the Lord's Supper with fellow believers, or in praying together. And while the same special, irreplaceable role could be said of each of these four Spiritual Disciplines within the church, it must also be said of *koinonia* that God chooses to touch lives through it unlike He does through anything else.

Don't forget that, by His Holy Spirit, God Himself lives within the genuinely converted members of your church. What's true of you is true of others—they themselves are not God, nor is He perfectly expressed through them. Nevertheless, He does live inside each Christian with whom you fellowship. He communicates Himself to you and gives grace through *koinonia* with Christians. He does not *save* us through fellowship; *saving* grace comes only through the life and death of Jesus Christ. But He does give us *sustaining* grace—spiritual strength for Christian living—via *koinonia*. And God's *koinonia* grace is not a duplicate of any other kind of His grace.

Since God gives grace and strength through fellowship, without fellowship you will be a spiritual weakling, fantasizing in private about your spiritual prowess, but powerless when it really counts. J. I. Packer concurs that the loss of fellowship means the loss of strength:

> I believe that one of the reasons why great sections of the modern church are so often sluggish and feeble, compared with our counterparts of one or two centuries ago, is that the secret of fellowship has been lost. Christ rebuked the Laodiceans for complacently supposing that they had all they needed when they were actually in a state of spiritual bankruptcy. I believe he would rebuke us for talking so glibly about the happy fellowship we have with each other when lack of fellowship really is one of our glaring shortcomings. A body in which the blood does not circulate properly is always below par, and fellowship corresponds to the circulation of the blood in the body of Christ. We gain strength through fellowship and we lose strength without it.[6]

Distance yourself from fellowship with the church, and there is a real sense in which you distance yourself from the grace of God. Cling to *koinonia*, and you stay close to where God loves to be gracious.

You Experience the Gifts and Grace Given to Others

God gives each Christian spiritual gifts that are to be used for the edification of the church. Peter teaches this in 1 Peter 4:10, "As each one has received a gift, minister it to one another, as good stewards of the manifold grace of God." Put another way, as God has gifted you for the purpose of ministering to others, so He has given gifts to others in your church that are to be used in ministry to you. Fellowship with the church is one of the chief channels for receiving what God intends from these gifted people.

The apostle Paul also speaks of Christians using their spiritual gifts together in a way that strengthens everyone in the church: "But, speaking the truth in love, [we] may grow up in all things into Him who is the head—Christ—from whom the whole body, joined and knit together by what *every joint supplies,* according to the effective working by which *every part does its share,* causes growth of the body for the edifying of itself in love" (Ephesians 4:15–16, italics added).

The Puritan theologian John Owen said of this passage, "It is the greatest and most glorious description of the communion of the saints that we have in the Scripture."[7] This "glorious description" is of a church body that grows stronger largely because of its *fellowship.* Do you see the sharing together, the *koinonia,* that *must* be occurring as "every joint, . . . each individual part . . . of the body" is involved in "the building up of itself in love"? (NASB).

Just in the past couple of weeks I have been built up stronger spiritually by the gifts of six other men with whom I have had fellowship. Sitting down with no more than two of them at a time, sometimes talking daily, I have had questions answered, insights provided, and resolve strengthened. All but one of the conversations was spontaneous and informal. In each case we simply asked questions of each other, such as,

"How do you know when the power of God has come upon a preacher?"

"What do you think this verse means?"

"If that's true, then what do we do with this other passage?"

"Am I weird, or do you ever think about these things?"

"Let me ask you what you think about something that I've been thinking about."

Each man has gifts and experience I do not have. It would be foolish and wasteful of me not to take advantage of this means of grace God has put all around me.

The same is true for you. Through Christians who are older and younger than you, through church members who are leaders and who are not, God has a spiritual smorgasbord called *koinonia* from which you are invited to feed and be strengthened.

Your Practice of the Spiritual Disciplines Is Encouraged

Christians wither without fellowship. One reason is that *koinonia* encourages us to practice those Spiritual Disciplines that promote spiritual health. Christians engaged in those disciplines that lead to godliness, such as the intake of God's Word, prayer, public and private worship, serving, etc., are examples and exhorters for us to do the same. When I am discouraged in prayer, for example, I hear someone talk about an exciting answer to prayer and that reinvigorates my own prayer life. But without fellowship to stimulate good spiritual habits we develop bad ones, the kind that lead to spiritual illness.

God used the writer of Hebrews to say to us, "Exhort one another daily, while it is called 'Today,' lest any of you be hardened through the deceitfulness of sin" (Hebrews 3:13). In order to "exhort one another daily" we must fellowship. What happens if we don't? Sin will deceive us and harden our hearts to many of the things of God, especially the Spiritual Disciplines.

Many discount *koinonia* but zealously practice certain Spiritual Disciplines in isolation, such as Bible study. Inevitably, however, they are spiritual eccentrics, hardened in other ways. They may carom from church to church like a lopsided pinball, smiling but never softening to share in the life of the body. Or with a face hardened by bitterness they may be long-nosed and sharp-tongued toward the "organized religion" of the church. Rejecting communion with the people of Jesus, they do not become more like Jesus.

In contrast are godly men and women such as Esther Edwards Burr, a daughter of Jonathan and Sarah Edwards, for whom *koinonia* was a sweet stimulus to her spirituality. In a biography of Jonathan

Edwards, Iain Murray said of Esther, "The occasions she seems to have appreciated most were the times of spiritual conversation." In the mid-1750s she wrote to a friend, describing a recent evening of fellowship:

> O my dear how Charming tis to set and hear such excellent persons convers on the experimentals of religion. It seemed like old times. . . . I esteem *religious Conversation* one of the best helps to keep up religion in the soul, excepting secret devotion, I don't know but the very best—Then what a lamentable thing that tis so neglected by God's own Children.[8]

What a lamentable thing indeed.

You Experience Love in Ways You Otherwise Cannot

Another of God's commands that cannot be obeyed without *koinonia* is "love one another" (John 13:34; 15:12, 17; 1 John 3:23). True, you can show love to people in their absence—doing a household chore normally done by your spouse, shoveling snow or mowing grass for your neighbor, running errands for a sick friend. But normally we give and receive love in person. So to love the people in your church, and to be loved by them, means you must spend time with them.

Of course, there's a risk inherent in *koinonia*. More than four decades of church life have taught me that, because of the nature of fellowship, no one can hurt a believer as deeply as a group of Christians. The more an individual holds in common with people, the more vulnerable he becomes to them. (Anyone who has ever been ridiculed by a brother or sister or had a spat with a spouse knows something of this.)

It's painful to do something for the church, then to have your motives misunderstood and be thought prideful. It's discouraging to have a ministry dream shot down by those you counted on for support. It's humiliating and disillusioning to discuss a problem in private only to hear that it's a "prayer request" spread throughout the church. It's disheartening to serve sacrificially and then receive only criticism in return. These things happen because the Christians in every fellowship are still sinners.

On the other hand, no one can love you like the brothers and sisters from your church can. At a funeral a week ago I watched a church care for a weary widow and her two children in a way usually unseen in the world. A collection of volunteers provided a sumptuous meal for her and for all her family and friends who came into town for the funeral. Couples visited quietly with the widow about her present and future financial needs. Others inquired about some practical needs she might have. Men put their arms around a wayward, twenty-year-old son and talked with him about the loss of his dad and about God's role in it all. Women of all ages hugged the four-year-old daughter and tearfully told her how much they love her and God loves her. Why did they do all this? Simply because she has a space on the church membership roll? No, because she is part of the *fellowship*. Her life is bound together with theirs. Her pain is their pain; her need is their opportunity. As a minister who has walked to and from the graveside with many people, I have seen this over and over. I've been on the receiving end of it myself when there have been deaths in my family.

When the world thinks you are worthless, no one can build you up as well as a church family can. No one is more likely to pick you up when you fall than those who share in the forgiveness of God with you. No one will listen more patiently and compassionately to the stories of your pain than the people of God in the church. No one will pray for God to heal you or guide you or provide for you as will the church. No one will stick by you when you are alone as the family of God will. No one will help you when you are in trouble or in need as those with whom you have *koinonia*.

Sure, exceptions can *often* be found in *every* church to each of these assertions. The bond of fellowship creates expectations that sometimes go unmet, just as the bond of matrimony does. And the sweeter the *koinonia*, the more bitter are its disappointments. But to adapt a proverb, it is much better to have fellowship and be hurt than never to fellowship at all. For you will find no greater love on a more consistent and enduring basis than through fellowship in a local church. Jesus Christ is in those people who are truly saved, and He will love you through them.

Even so, fellowship is much like a bank in this regard: You must make deposits if you want to make withdrawals. *Koinonia*, by definition, isn't a one-way relationship. If you want people to be there for you, you need to be there for them. Just because you share a pew with someone doesn't mean you share life with him. Attendance and fellowship are not the same thing.

Two of my dear friends are Jim and Mary. They cared for Mary's mom in their home during the final months of her fight with cancer. No one ever did a better and more loving job in these circumstances than they, but such times are exhausting for anyone. While the church family would never claim perfection in its response, nevertheless I repeatedly saw people eager for an opportunity to bring meals, run errands, take a shift at the bedside, or do whatever they could to help.

The eagerness was a reflexive response to how Jim and Mary had shared their lives with others for years. Jim was one of the best at making household and automotive repairs for others. Mary was always the first to come to the hospital to sit all day if necessary with someone who had a loved one in surgery or to volunteer to run errands for new moms. But they weren't only concerned for outward needs. In the midst of all their practical need-meeting, they sought to talk about the simultaneous needs of the soul and to pray with those to whom they ministered. Those who make the biggest contributions to *koinonia* tend to receive the greatest outpourings of love in return.

MORE SCRIPTURAL TRUTHS ABOUT FELLOWSHIP

The need for fellowship with the church is undeniable.

Spiritual people need to talk about spiritual things. As Jerry Bridges put it in *True Fellowship* (the best book I've found on the subject), "Spiritual fellowship is not a luxury, but a necessity, vital to our spiritual growth and health."[9] J. I. Packer concurs: "The fellowship of sharing with one another what we have received from the Lord is a *spiritual necessity*. For God has not made us self-sufficient. We are not made so we can keep going on our own."[10]

A pastor went to visit a church member who had been neglecting fellowship. The man invited him in, and they both sat down by the fireplace. Without speaking, the pastor looked thoughtfully into the fire for several minutes. Then, taking the iron poker, he pulled one of the red-hot coals to the front edge of the hearth. Soon it lost its glowing warmth and became dark and cool. Silently the pastor pushed the coal back into the company of the other embers and it quickly returned to its former strength.

"I see what you mean, Pastor," the man admitted. "I'll be back this Sunday."

The strength of your spiritual fire is related to the fellowship you have with the body of Christ. You will not be able to maintain your spiritual fervency without the spiritual fuel God supplies through *koinonia*.

The neglect of fellowship with the church is sinful.

It's not just that you are missing out on blessings if you neglect fellowship; it's also sin to shun *koinonia*. Hebrews 10:24–25 has application not only to church attendance but also to fellowship with the church when it says, "And let us consider one another in order to stir up love and good works, not forsaking the assembling of ourselves together, as is the manner of some, but exhorting one another, and so much the more as you see the Day approaching." To forsake assembling together and encouraging one another is a sinful violation of this command.

How *do* we assemble together and encourage one another? You can't do it only by sitting in worship together, even though that is crucial. A lot of this encouragement obviously has to involve face-to-face interaction. I don't mean that we must gather in small groups for "encouragement meetings." Rather, through the infinite ways of having fellowship we can fulfill God's benevolent command to assemble and encourage one another.

During my years of ministry I've heard many reasons that professing Christians cut the cords of *koinonia* with the church. But none of them sound like something Jesus would say. As John Wesley, founder of Methodism, said with a prophetic edge, "There is nothing more unchristian than a solitary Christian."[11]

The privilege of fellowship with the church is costly.

Earlier I called your attention to 1 John 1:3, which declares that the foundation of our fellowship with Christians on earth is our fellowship with God in heaven. "That which we have seen and heard we declare to you," writes John, "that you also may have fellowship with us; and truly our fellowship is with the Father and with His Son Jesus Christ." Remember what it cost God to provide you with this privilege. The privilege of participation in eternal life and glory, as well as the privilege of the best relationships in the world, were paid for by the death of God's Son.

If it cost God so dearly to provide the privilege of fellowship, it may cost you to enjoy it. One cost is time. You may live far from a church where you can find true fellowship. To share your life with that body of Christians will require more travel time than you'd like. But a good church is worth it.

Fellowship may cost you some initiative or hospitality. You may need to take the lead to make fellowship intentional. As a pastor I stumbled into something that many at our church enjoyed. After the evening worship service one Sunday night a month, we met in a home for what was called a "Fellowship/Theological Discussion Meeting." It was modeled somewhat on the Friday night meetings with a similar title in London's Westminster Chapel where Dr. Martyn Lloyd-Jones was pastor for thirty years.[12] The purpose of the meeting was to have fellowship by discussing theological questions.

I chaired each meeting and began by asking if anyone had questions about the sermons of that day. Usually one or more did, but if not I asked for questions regarding any recent sermons I had delivered. If there still was no response I inquired, "What theological or biblical questions have been on your mind lately?" With only two exceptions did we ever get this far without starting a discussion. In the event of such situations I always came prepared with a couple of questions for us to consider. After an hour I would read the day's selection from a devotional book and pray. That provided an opportunity for those who needed to leave to go home, while the rest of us would get refills on refreshments and start again. After another hour or so I would pray once more and the fellowshipers would regretfully begin their good-byes.

Knowing that we were going to do nothing but talk about God and the things of God, we never failed to have an overflow crowd— teenagers to senior adults. I can remember times where people sat in twos up a flight of stairs while others stood in the kitchen and dining room. Such fellowship cost some time, some leadership, and, for the hostess, some hospitality. Looking back on it though, I think it was one of the most fruitful and unifying ministries of the church.

For a variety of reasons, a churchwide meeting like this may be impractical in your situation. However, you might be able to initiate a gathering of friends, a class, or another group from church and have a similar time of fellowship. Perhaps it might simply be two or three other individuals who would meet you for breakfast or coffee on a regular basis. Here are a few fellowship-prompting questions you could use:

- What have you seen God do lately?

- What do you feel good about right now in the spiritual area of your life?

- Where are you having slow-going right now spiritually?

- How is your _____ ministry going? (For example, a ministry as a Sunday school teacher.)

- How are you doing with the Spiritual Disciplines?

- What's the most meaningful thing that has happened to you since we last talked?

- What's the most important decision facing you in the near future?

- Have you read anything recently that has helped you spiritually?

- What's something the Lord has been teaching you lately?

- How can I pray for you?

The pursuit of fellowship with the church is worthwhile.

The cohesion of *koinonia* is what we were made for. I want to emphasize this again to two kinds of people I mentioned at the beginning. The first is the person who has groped from group to group, looking for fellowship in independent Bible studies, men's or women's movements, parachurch organizations, service groups, or other worthwhile ministries—everywhere but the local church. Don't believe that the world or even Christian organizations will ever develop a better place for soul-knitting relationships than the one Jesus died to create. The Bible says, "A man who has friends must himself be friendly" (Proverbs 18:24). As with friendship, fellowship requires some initiative. Soul-knitting relationships don't happen just by walking in the door of the church building. Seek fellowship among the people of God and you will find it. You will also find that it's worth the effort.

The other kind of individual I want to address is the one who wants Christ but not the church. He or she "doesn't like crowds," considers himself or herself more of a loner than one who mixes well with people, and simply doesn't think fellowship is necessary. A Bible, some good books, and perhaps a TV or radio preacher and the Christian isolationist is content. Maybe a little venturing into relationships via computer too, but that's as close as this person wants to get to "assembling together" for "fellowship." You can't live the Christian life alone. Jesus didn't. There is no Christlikeness in isolationism.

British theologian Alister McGrath summarizes well: "The Christian is not meant to be, nor called to be, a radical and solitary romantic, wandering in isolated loneliness through the world; rather, the Christian is called to be a member of a community."[13] That community is the local church.

CHAPTER ELEVEN

WHY PRAY WITH THE CHURCH?

· · · · · · · ✦ · · · · · · ·

Brethren, we shall never see much change
for the better in our churches in general
till the prayer meeting occupies a higher
place in the esteem of Christians.

Charles H. Spurgeon

Most people pray. In fact, most people pray often, or at least they say they do. In the United States, nine out of ten people say they pray to God. Four out of five adults who pray say that prayer is a *regular* part of their lives. And of those adults who *ever* pray to God, almost six out of ten (58 percent) claim they pray every day, and most of those say they pray more than once a day. Even two-thirds of those who never go to church say that they pray.[1]

Yet with all this individual prayer, there seems to be much less *group* prayer. In the Western half of the world, and particularly in America, the independent spirit prevails over the *inter*dependent spirit. The spirit of the discoverer, the frontiersman, the pioneer heading west with all his worldly goods in a covered wagon, the lone farming family on the prairie with no neighbors for miles, the cowboy on the open range, the space explorer, the entrepreneur—this spirit is a major influence on our American view of the Christian life.

In his book *Praying for One Another,* Pastor Gene Getz observes,

The hallmark of Western civilization has been rugged individualism. Because of our philosophy of life, we are used to the personal pronouns I and my and me. We have not been taught to think in terms of we and our and us. Consequently we "individualize" many references to corporate experience in the New Testament, thus often emphasizing personal prayer, personal Bible study, personal evangelism, and personal Christian maturity and growth. The facts are that more is said in the Book of Acts and the Epistles about corporate prayer, corporate learning of biblical truth, corporate evangelism, and corporate Christian maturity and growth than about the personal aspects of these Christian disciplines. Don't misunderstand. Both are intricately related. But the personal dimensions of Christianity are difficult to maintain and practice consistently unless they grow out of a proper corporate experience on a regular basis. . . . The emphasis in the scriptural record is clearly on corporate prayer being the context in which personal prayer becomes meaningful.[2]

Let's look at the scriptural record and see why it is important and beneficial to pray with the church.

PRAYER WITH THE CHURCH IS A MARK OF NEW TESTAMENT CHRISTIANITY

The first Christians were men and women of prayer. But their reputation as praying people does not come from their individual prayer lives nearly as much as from their congregational prayer. Let's return to Acts 2:42 and that first description of church life in Jerusalem. We find there that when God's people were full of His Spirit, this was the result: "And they continued steadfastly in the apostles' doctrine and fellowship, in the breaking of bread, and in *prayers*" (italics added).

Don't think of this merely as an observation of the quaint habits of Christians long ago in a culture far away. If there is distance between the practice of these believers and that of many Christians today, it isn't just the separation of centuries and cultures. As the early part of Acts 2 relates, God had come powerfully upon these people. When He did, one of the results was a magnetic devotion to praying with the others who had the Spirit of God. Praying with the church is what Christians eagerly do when they are full of God. So if we feel no compulsion for intercession with God's people, perhaps that alone should prompt us to pray for God to come among us as He did upon these believers.

If you have ever read the book of Acts, you know it is impossible to imagine the members of the church in Jerusalem *not* gathering to pray with each other. This was Christianity in the New Testament. Congregational prayerlessness ought to be just as unimaginable for us in our own churches. If we want to see in our churches what they saw in theirs, we should pray with our churches as they prayed with theirs.

E. M. Bounds, author of many enduring books on prayer, maintained, "The life, power, and glory of the church is prayer. . . . Without it, the church is lifeless and powerless."[3] The churches we read about in the New Testament were anything but lifeless and powerless. They were churches where the people made a priority of prayer.

PRAYER WITH THE CHURCH BRINGS THE POWER OF UNITED PRAYER

This is taught in one of the best-known, but most often misapplied, passages on prayer, Matthew 18:19–20. There Jesus said, "Again I say to you that if two of you agree on earth concerning anything that they ask, it will be done for them by My Father in heaven. For where two or three are gathered together in My name, I am there in the midst of them."

This promise is frequently quoted in regard to prayer, but rarely in its context. The context is a passage on church discipline. Jesus has (in verses 15–18) been giving instructions on how an individual Christian within the church, then how the church as a whole, should respond when there is known, persistent, and unrepentant sin by a member of the church family. In verses 19–20 Jesus gives the assurance that where two or three (as in the "two or three witnesses" in verse 16) gather to pray and deal with someone in the way He has ordained, He will be with them. Incidentally, this is a precious promise for those courageous enough to attempt obedience to Christ here, for there may be threats against them, and they may feel quite lonely and in need of this reminder.

Biblical, loving church discipline is almost non-existent in the evangelical church in America today. Many who pretend not to see it in Scripture also fail to see the relationship between discipline and the church's prayer life. To quote Bounds again, "Let it be noted with emphasis that a church which is careless of discipline will be careless in praying. A church which tolerates evildoers in its communion, will cease to pray, will cease to pray in agreement."[4]

There is, however, one word in this verse that makes it broad enough to encompass all corporate prayer. Notice that Jesus says in verse 19 that "if two of you agree on earth concerning *anything* that they ask, it will be done for them by My Father in heaven" (italics added). Thus we can take this promise and apply it to any united prayer, not just prayer regarding church discipline.

But why is this promise necessary? Doesn't the Bible teach the omnipresence of God, that God is present everywhere? Yes, clearly it does. Jesus said in Matthew 28:20, "I am with you *always,* even to the end of the age" (italics added).

Jesus is saying more in Matthew 18:19–20 than that He is present when two or more pray together. He is giving us an added promise of power that comes when God's people unite in their requests to Him. Of course, this is a unity of spirit and purpose that goes beyond mere agreement of the terms of the request. United prayer is more than sitting in the same location with another and praying about the same thing.

In his discipleship course *PrayerLife,* T. W. Hunt recounts how he learned the difference between mutual prayer and united prayer, and the greater power in the latter:

> My wife and I established our family altar before we were married. Now, in our mid-fifties, Laverne and I were rejoicing that we had seen a lifetime of mutual prayer answered. Our son-in-law was as godly as we had prayed for him to be. Our daughter was totally committed to the Lordship of Christ. They were godly, praying Christians. Our grandchildren were already demonstrating the fruit of much prayer. We felt that our family devotions lacked nothing, and we were each growing in the Lord. There was much thanksgiving in our home.
>
> Then Laverne was stricken with cancer. Two things began happening immediately. The first was an instinctive turning to God in deeper dimensions. Grief is often a father to new insights. . . .

The second thing that happened to us was that we drew closer together.

At this point Dr. Hunt begins outlining dramatic answers to prayer that they began to see, some that related to Laverne's condition and some that did not. And although it had not occurred at the writing of his book, from my relationship with him I know that such answers continued for them, even to the eventual, unexpected removal of all signs of cancer from Laverne for a period now approaching ten years. So his conclusion is even more powerful now than when he wrote it: "One night as we were marveling over what seemed to be happening in our prayers together, we were able to articulate a new principle for united prayer: *The closer the bond, the more powerful the prayer; the higher the unity, the greater the authority in prayer.*"5

What is true for united prayer between a husband and wife is also true for united prayer with the church. There is a potential for power and authority in corporate prayer that we forsake—*while at the same time longing for answered prayer*—when we forsake united prayer with the people of God.

UNITED PRAYER IS LINKED WITH THE EFFECTIVENESS OF THE GOSPEL AND THE CHURCH

Persecution had come because of the gospel. The church's top leaders—Peter and John—had been arrested and had spent a night in jail. The next day the most powerful of the Jewish authorities interrogated them and "commanded them not to speak at all nor teach in the name of Jesus" (Acts 4:18). When the two apostles were released, the church gathered to hear their report. What was the church's response to the threat? "So when they heard that, they raised their voice to God with one accord" (Acts 4:24).

This is no surprise. But what did they pray? For protection and removal of the persecution? No, but rather, "Now, Lord, look on their threats, and grant to Your servants that with all boldness they may speak Your word" (v. 29).

What was the Lord's reply? "And when they had prayed, the place where they were assembled together was shaken; and they were all filled with the Holy Spirit, and they spoke the word of God with boldness" (4:31). The result was that the gospel and the church spread even more.

T. W. Hunt adds:

> If we examine the expansion of the church in the Book of Acts and look at its prayers as recorded in Acts and the Epistles, we see convincing proof of the power of prayer. The early church had innumerable obstacles—Christianity was unknown, and it was opposed by the authorities wherever it spread, it suffered constantly from false accusations and rumors, and it tended to attract the lower classes. Yet by the end of the first century, it had spread in exactly the geographic pattern commissioned by Jesus—Jerusalem, Judea, Samaria, and the "uttermost parts of the earth," points in Europe and Asia Minor far distant from its seedbed. . . . This rapid geographical and ideological shift could have been accomplished only by supernatural forces. The instrument of expansion was the church, and the force the church was using was prayer.[6]

From its earliest days, the church has always been at its best when its people have knelt together. It is very important for us to work in the church so it can prosper. It's imperative that we give so that the needs of the church can be met. But our work and our money can never do for the church what only the power of God can do. And the power of God never comes upon the church as it does when the church prays.

The Preacher and His Sermons Need Your Prayer

The kind of united prayer that the Bible links with the effectiveness of the gospel and the church is not simply general prayers of blessing for the church, but prayer for both the preachers and the preaching of the gospel.

For example, if any man could have successfully proclaimed the message of Jesus Christ in his own power it was the apostle Paul. He has been acclaimed as one of the mental giants of history. He had one of the best and most intellectually rigorous educations of his day. He became a Pharisee of the Jews, which would have required superior skills with the Old Testament text and memorization of huge sections of Scripture. Then, at his conversion, he was confronted by an appearance of the risen Jesus Christ Himself.

During his ministry Paul saw the Lord work countless miracles through his hands. Angels appeared to him, the Lord spoke to him through visions, and he was even allowed to become the only known human spoken of in Scripture to be taken to heaven for a visit. He was a mighty apostle, preacher, and missionary. If anyone should have ever felt little sense of dependence on the church, it would have been Paul. And yet, over and over he pleads with local churches, "Pray for me."

Notice how he relied upon the prayers of these local churches for the effectiveness of his ministry:

- Now I beg you, brethren, through the Lord Jesus Christ, and through the love of the Spirit, that you strive together with me in *prayers to God for me*, that I may be delivered from those in Judea who do not believe, and that my service for Jerusalem may be acceptable to the saints, that I may come to you with joy by the will of God, and may be refreshed together with you. (Romans 15:30–32, italics added)

- . . . you also helping together in *prayer for us* . . . (2 Corinthians 1:11, italics added)

- *Praying always* with all prayer and supplication in the Spirit, being watchful to this end with all perseverance and supplication for all the saints—and *for m*e, that utterance may be given to me, that I may open my mouth boldly to make known the mystery of the gospel, for which I am an ambassador in chains; that in it I may speak boldly, as I ought to speak. (Ephesians 6:18–20, italics added)

- Meanwhile *praying also for us*, that God would open to us a door for the word, to speak the mystery of Christ, for which I am also in chains, that I may make it manifest, as I ought to speak. (Colossians 4:3–4, italics added)

- Finally, brethren, *pray for us*, that the word of the Lord may run swiftly and be glorified. (2 Thessalonians 3:1, italics added)

E. M. Bounds soberly asks, "If Paul was so dependent on the prayers of God's saints to give his ministry success, how much greater the necessity that the prayers of God's saints be centered on the ministry of today!"[7]

The church must pray unitedly for its preacher so that "the word of the Lord may run swiftly and be glorified." The members of the church—people such as you—must pray together if the church is to have any lasting fruit for all the time and money it has invested in the Lord's service. Why have a church, why be part of a church that has little or no power to change lives? Yet such power comes from God alone, and He gives it only to churches that pray. So if you will not pray with your church, what lasting benefits can you expect from your church?

Prayer Should Be Made for Revival and Reformation

Beginning with the power of the Holy Spirit that came upon the followers of Jesus as they prayed with one accord (Acts 2:1) on the day of Pentecost, the most dynamic movements of reformation and revival God has sent to His church have exploded from united prayer. Here are brief examples from several centuries and countries.

The beginning of the First Great Awakening is usually traced to the preaching of Jonathan Edwards's sermon, "Sinners in the Hands of an Angry God." He was away from his congregation at Northampton, Massachusetts (which would later become synonymous with the awakening), and preaching at Enfield. More than a hundred years later, in *The Power of Prayer,* Samuel Prime recorded:

> The revival which began at Enfield, Mass, on the 8th of July, 1741, under a sermon preached by the elder President Edwards, on the words *Their feet shall slide in due time*, has long been regarded as one of the most powerful on record. The impression of eternal things was awful and overwhelming. Many, knowing nothing of the history of that work, are surprised at so great effects from one sermon. But the fact is, that some Christians in that vicinity had become alarmed lest God should in anger pass by that church, and had spent the whole of the preceding night in prayer.[8]

Even more dramatic is the story of corporate prayer that preceded the 1858 revival that started in New York, swept across America, leaped to the British Isles, then spread to countries throughout the world. Jeremiah Lanphier was an inner-city missionary associated with the North Dutch Reformed Church located on Fulton Street in New York City. As he prayed for God's direction in his work, the thought came to him that a noontime prayer meeting might be beneficial to businessmen. Invitations were distributed, and at noon on September 27, 1857, Lanphier opened the door to a third-story lecture room of the church building. For half an hour Lanphier prayed alone. At 12:30 the step of a solitary individual was heard upon the stairs. Then another, and another, until six men had gathered for a brief time of prayer.

The second meeting was held a week later with twenty attending. The next week attendance doubled to forty and the group decided to make the prayer meeting a daily event. On October 14 Lanphier noted that more than one hundred were present, including many who did not know Christ and who were asking how to be saved.

Within two months the daily gathering filled all three of the church's large lecture rooms. By mid-spring there were noontime prayer meetings at twenty different locations across the city. Soon prayer meetings and conversions began to multiply in other cities. In some areas prayer meetings that began with six or seven people increased to six and seven thousand. Within months the impact was felt from coast to coast. Sometimes as many as fifty thousand people per week were being converted. It is estimated that out of a population of less than 30 million, at least a million Americans professed faith in Christ in one year.

As Christians in the U.K. heard these accounts, a similar movement of prayer began. When the power of God fell there in 1859, 10 percent of the Irish, Scots, and Welsh populations are believed to have been converted. It all started, and was sustained, by the power of the Holy Spirit in response to united prayer.

From 1949 to 1952, the wind of God blew in hurricane force across the Isle of Lewis, largest of the Hebrides Islands of Scotland. One unforgettable night, people came under deep conviction of sin during the preaching of the gospel. From every part of the crowded building came cries for mercy. Voices of those in spiritual distress could be heard outside in the road. A man beneath the pulpit wept aloud, "O God, hell is too good for me!" As the meeting concluded and the last person was about to leave, a young man began to pray. People started returning to the building, and the meeting resumed and did not end until 4:00 A.M. Just then someone came to the preacher and said excitedly, "Come with me! There's a crowd of people outside the police station; they are weeping and in awful distress. We don't know what's wrong with them, but they are calling for someone to come and pray with them."

The minister later described the scene: "I saw a sight I never thought possible. Something I shall never forget. Under a starlit sky, men and women were kneeling everywhere, by the roadside, outside the cottages, even behind the peat stacks, crying for God to have mercy on them!"

How did this begin? The united prayers of the people of the church. For months a small group of men and their minister had met in a little wooden barn three nights a week to ask God for revival.[9]

"It is true that revival is the absolute prerogative of a sovereign God," asserts South African Erroll Hulse. "Yet in a strange way His purposes are joined to the prayers of His people."[10]

Believers Need to Pray for Evangelism and Missions

For the same reasons that it's important for us to pray with others for the success of the gospel and for revival, we should also pray with them for the proclamation of the gospel and the work of the Spirit on the mission field. In 1727, a community of believers in Saxony who came to be known as Herrnhut (the Lord's Watch), started a round-the-clock prayer vigil that continued nonstop for one hundred years. As they prayed, the Lord began to give them a missionary passion. By 1792, sixty-five years into the prayer watch, three hundred missionaries had gone out from them to the ends of the earth.[11] By the time they had prayed one hundred years, this one group had sent out more missionaries than all Protestants had sent out in the previous two centuries.[12]

The contemporary church has technology, psychology, and marketing, but do we know anything of the power of God upon our preaching and ministry that the people in these stories experienced? The Bible and the testimony of church history say that, despite how outdated it may seem, the effectiveness of the gospel and of the church are inseparably related to the united prayers of God's people.

YOU NEED OTHERS TO PRAY FOR YOU

Some of the things you seek from God may not be given except when others in your church pray for you. For instance, the Bible gives instructions in James 5:14, 16 about what a Christian should do when he or she is sick. "Is anyone among you sick? Let him call for the elders of the church, and let them pray over him, anointing him with oil in the name of the Lord. . . . Confess your trespasses to one another, and pray for one another, that you may be healed." There are many controversies surrounding this text that I will not address, but there is no dispute about this being prayer with others from the church. The sick person's responsibility here is to "call for the elders of the *church.*" Notice also the instruction "pray for one another" in verse 16. Apparently there are some blessings God gives only to those who humble themselves to say that they need others in the church and their prayers. There may be some things you are praying for right now that you will not receive unless the church or a group within the church prays for you.

Earlier we saw where that spiritual giant, the apostle Paul, felt a profound need for the prayers of others. More importantly, even the Lord Jesus Christ Himself asked for the prayers of others. As He went heavy heartedly into the privacy of the Garden of Gethsemane, He said to Peter, James, and John, " 'My soul is exceedingly sorrowful, even to death. Stay here and watch with Me.' . . . Then He came to the disciples and found them sleeping, and said to Peter, 'What? Could you not watch with Me one hour? Watch and pray, lest you enter into temptation. The spirit indeed is willing, but the flesh is weak' " (Matthew 26:38, 40–41). If Jesus asked a group of friends to pray for Him, then you need the prayers of others also.

Western individualism and self-sufficiency chafes at this. We want to think that if our own prayer life is strong enough then we'll manage just fine. In other words, somehow it seems a sign of spiritual weakness if we have to ask others to pray for us. But let's not try to be more "spiritual" than Jesus. If He requested prayer support, only pride will keep us from doing the same.

However, there are many who are quick to *ask* for prayer from people in the church and who will even pray for others in return, but who will not commit themselves to pray *with* these same brothers and sisters. This is neither normal nor healthy Christianity. Beware of the spiritual independence of a completely privatized prayer life. The Bible tells us to pray *together*. As the nineteenth century South African missionary leader and devotional writer, Andrew Murray, helps us see, "Nothing would be more unnatural than that the children of a family should always meet their father separately, but never in the united expression of their desires or their love."[13]

BECOMING COMMITTED TO CORPORATE PRAYER

Is corporate prayer important to you?

If congregational or small group prayer isn't part of your Christian life, there's a problem. Private-only prayer is not New Testament Christianity. Prayer with others from the body of believers was one of the four marks of the church in Acts 2:42. Some say they don't pray with groups because they are too self-conscious when praying aloud with others. This verse doesn't say they all prayed *aloud,* but it does mean that they prayed *together*. If you are unwilling to pray with others, you are too independent spiritually.

Will you become an active part of the prayer life of your church?

There are several ways to do that:

You can participate in congregational prayer. If your church has a designated meeting for prayer, attend and participate. Perhaps you don't have the freedom or fluency in public prayer that some enjoy. There is no requirement as to the length of prayers. Begin with one-sentence prayers of thanksgiving for specific blessings. Soon you'll find yourself saying more. And when others pray, participate by listening carefully and saying "Amen" to God in your heart when they express something that is a desire of yours as well.

You can volunteer for the prayer ministry of your church. Many churches have a ministry group that is devoted not only to praying, but also to mobilizing the church for prayer. They may oversee the church's prayer room, a prayer chain, and/or a variety of other ministries that fall under their guidance. If your church doesn't have a prayer ministry, ask your pastor if you could start one. Most pastors would be delighted at the idea.

You can start or join a small prayer group. You may have a few friends within the church who would be willing to meet with you before work during a weekday, before church on Sunday, or some other time for weekly prayer.

If you long for more of the blessing of God upon the preaching of the Scriptures and the ministry of your church, and for more of God's grace on your own life, then meet with your fellow believers and pray for it. Will God reject the united prayers of His people who ask Him to bless His own Word and work? In the midst of the contemporary church's search for increasingly sophisticated methods, let's not forget the pleasure God takes in the confluence of His children's voices. As the Puritan John Flavel reminds us, "God sometimes stands upon a number of voices, for the carrying of some public mercy, because he delighteth in the harmony of many praying souls."[14]

CHAPTER TWELVE

WHY LEARN IN THE CHURCH?

· · · · · · · · ✦ · · · · · · · ·

The institution of the church is a necessary,
helpful, God-given, and God-ordained means
of spiritual growth and development.
It is meant to be there—and it is meant to be used.

Alister E. McGrath

You've probably never heard of men such as William Friedman, Frank Rowlett, and Arthur Levenson, but they made dramatic contributions which helped to win World War II. They were cryptanalysts, and their work as codebreakers was unheralded and virtually unknown for fifty years afterward. Without their efforts, the war would have lasted much longer.

For instance, the turning point in the Pacific theater was the naval Battle of Midway. The Americans knew from intercepted messages that the Japanese were going to attack, but they didn't know where. Many thought the target would be the Aleutian Islands off the Alaskan coast. Their suspicions were confirmed when a Japanese fleet was seen steaming Alaska-ward. But American Admiral Chester Nimitz gambled and kept the Pacific fleet's only three aircraft carriers and his main force near Midway Island, primarily upon clues given to him by a handful of codebreakers at nearby Pearl Harbor.

As it turned out, the force sailing to the Aleutians was a decoy. Without the information given to him by the cryptanalysts, Nimitz would have split his fleet and almost certainly lost Midway and the Hawaiian Islands, leaving the West Coast of the U.S. without any outer defenses. Although few battles were as consequential as Midway, the outcome of many others was also decided by what was learned from the codebreakers.

The codebreakers of all the Allied countries in World War II were successful because they learned from one another. U.S. and British codebreakers worked intimately, sharing keys or potential keys to deciphering a code as soon as they were discovered. Even within each Allied government, no one could crack a code by himself. Not even the head of American cryptanalysis, William Friedman, who has been called by historians the most brilliant cryptanalyst ever, worked alone. Friedman was part of a team that collaborated for years and learned to interpret the meanings of encrypted foreign messages together.[1]

God has *not* spoken to us cryptically in the sixty-six books which make up the Bible. Any person who has the Holy Spirit (that is, any Christian) has both the ability to understand the Scriptures and the right to interpret them for himself. This is taught in 1 John 2:27—"But the anointing which you have received from Him abides in you, and you do not need that anyone teach you."

However, the New Testament also makes clear that God has given teachers to the church. We further know that every believer has much to learn about our infinite God and His written Word. And though we have the right to interpret the Bible individually, we also have the responsibility to interpret it properly. Christians have been given the Holy Spirit, who opens our eyes to know God through Jesus Christ and to understand the Scriptures, but we all have a tendency toward subjectivity. In other words, despite the competence the Spirit provides to all believers for knowing God and His Word, He doesn't grant *complete* knowledge of God to us or an *infallible* understanding of Scripture.

Because of this natural weakness, there is much about the Lord and His ways, His will for our lives, and the Bible which will seem like an encrypted enigma to us without the help of some fellow "codebreakers." The codebreakers from whom God intends us to learn are our Christian brothers and sisters in our local church.

The Bible gives several reasons why you should learn in the church.

THE CHURCH IS "THE PILLAR AND GROUND OF THE TRUTH" OF GOD

In 1 Timothy 3:15 the Spirit of God guided the apostle Paul to describe the church as "the church of the living God, the pillar and ground of the truth." The church, including the expressions of the church locally, is like a pillar that supports something above it. And that which the church lifts up is the truth of God. God created the church and gave it the responsibility to elevate His Word. So anyone who is not learning in the church distances himself from the only pillar in the world which upholds the indispensable truth of God.

While writing this chapter I had a conversation with a young man who had grown up in the church, but had stopped attending. His college philosophy class had influenced him to consider other religions, and he began questioning some things he'd always believed. Another man from the church and I reminded him of the uniqueness of Jesus Christ and His claims. Unlike other religions, we noted, which are built on principles that can stand independently of the religion's founder, Christianity rises or falls upon Christ. We discussed with him the singularity and exclusivity of the message of the Christian church and the factual evidences—chiefly the resurrection of Christ—to support its claims. As he heard the truth that God has revealed for us in Scripture, the clouds of doubt began to dissipate. His help came when he was willing to learn in the church, "the pillar and ground of the truth."

The world is not going to uphold the truth of God for you. It is in a faithful, Bible-teaching church that you will be taught the truth—the truth about yourself, the truth about God, the truth about your need to know God through Jesus Christ, the truth about living most wisely and abundantly, and the truth about Judgment and eternity.

In Hebrews 5:12 the author admonished his readers because so many of the things of God were still beyond their comprehension. He wrote, "For though by this time you ought to be teachers, you need someone to teach you again the first principles of the oracles of God; and you have come to need milk and not solid food." Maybe you are like these Christians—you've been a believer for quite a while, but you haven't learned the things of God as you should. You would have to admit, "I understand some of the Bible, but much of it reads like a message in code."

For instance, do you know what the gospel is; that is, could you write it plainly and concisely in a letter to a friend who asked, "How can I become a Christian?" Do you know the biblical evidences of salvation? Do you know how to pray? Do you know what your spiritual gift is? Do you know the attributes of God? Do you know the great doctrines of salvation—election, regeneration, justification, sanctification, glorification? Or are all these things as code words to you?

No one knows these things naturally, and the world doesn't teach you about them. The world doesn't even *use* many of these words. As J. I. Packer put it in the title of a book, these are *God's Words*, they have to do with eternal life, and the fact that only the church talks about them underscores the reason you need to learn in the church.

The church is a tainted trustee of these things, but it does have the truth. It is an imperfect messenger, but it has a perfect message. The church of Jesus Christ is the pillar which proclaims the message of the Man who said, "I am *the* way, *the* truth, and *the* life. No one comes to the Father *except* through *Me*" (John 14:6, italics added). Stand afar from the pillar of God's truth and you will likely stand far from understanding His truth well.

CHRISTIAN DISCIPLESHIP IS MORE THAN ACADEMICS

Some will say, "I don't need the church to get the truth of God. I can study the Bible on my own. I can learn from Bible teachers on Christian radio, TV, and tapes. I can take correspondence courses or use my computer to study theology online. I can do a number of things like these without learning at a local church." Not long ago someone who had stopped coming to church told me that she was doing fine spiritually because through radio she listened to seven sermons a day. Others have informed me they don't need to learn in the church because they go to seminary classes every day. Surely anyone who takes in such a torrential amount of truth doesn't need to learn from the church, does he?

For starters, I wonder if those who neglect the local church for these reasons ever hear a radio sermon or seminary lecture on Hebrews 10:25 about "not forsaking the assembling of ourselves together, as is the manner of some."

Additionally, there's more to discipleship than the intellectual part. The "academic side" is essential; after all, the only way to be transformed is "by the renewing of your mind" (Romans 12:2). To grow in Christlikeness we must hear and process the truth. But Christian discipleship is more than mastering information.

Paul writes about this in Colossians 1:28 as he explains the purpose of his own ministry: "And we proclaim Him, admonishing every man and teaching every man with all wisdom, that we may present every man complete in Christ (NASB)." As with Paul, our goal is not merely "teaching," that is, transmitting facts about Christ and the Bible from one mind or notebook to another. Rather, teaching takes place "that [so that, for this purpose] we may present every man perfect in Christ Jesus." And by learning in the local church you learn more broadly and experientially than you learn from Christian radio, tapes, and so forth, although they can be extremely valuable supplemental sources. Learning in the church allows for dialogue, modeling, hands-on practice, and other means of learning which must accompany and complement the academic side of discipleship.

This is why it's both unwise and unbiblical to think of a minister on radio or television as your pastor. The only way he can pastor you is by talking to you. As important as solid teaching is, and as much as you may enjoy his style, pastoring is more than teaching. He could never be the kind of example to the flock (including you) that Scripture commands pastors to be (1 Peter 5:2–3), for you never see or hear him except in the artificial environment of the media. He could not say, as did the apostle Paul, "The things which you learned and received and heard and *saw* in me, these do, and the God of peace will be with you" (Philippians 4:9, italics added). He could never take you and others he "pastors" with him as he witnesses or ministers in hospitals and homes. Nor could you ever watch him apply the truth to his own life, especially in the day-to-day situations of which life is made. He could not hold you accountable through spiritual discipline. Learning in the church is always richer and better balanced than learning alone or through media.

If you are a serious-minded student of Scripture, of course you can get more thorough and concentrated teaching in a short time if you attend seminary than you are likely to get in the same length of time in a church. That's what seminaries are for. A seminary curriculum may require more time from you in one day than you would normally give to the church in a week. Seminaries are able to teach on a higher academic level than churches, for a church must often teach both well and poorly educated people at the same time. Seminaries can also require students to read books, write papers, take tests, and so on. But we still need to learn in the church, because Christian learning is more than just acquiring data.

GOD HAS PLACED GIFTED PEOPLE
IN THE CHURCH TO TEACH YOU

The New Testament passages on spiritual gifts tell us that God has placed gifted people in the church to teach us. Notice the term "pastors and teachers" in Ephesians 4:11–12: "And He Himself gave some to be apostles, some prophets, some evangelists, and some pastors and teachers, for the equipping of the saints for the work of ministry, for the edifying of the body of Christ." God has given gifted people to the church to equip the church, to do the work of the church, and to build up the church.

Romans 12:7, another spiritual gifts text, says that some within the church have the gift of teaching. The text refers to "he who teaches." Not all teachers are pastors, or even "official" teachers with classes in the church. But God has placed in the church people with the gift of teaching so that He might teach us through them.

Jonathan Edwards wrote about how those who are not teachers should respond to those who are:

> If God have [sic] made it the business of some to be teachers, it
> will follow, that he hath made it the business of others to be learn-
> ers; for teachers and learners are correlates, one of which was
> never intended to be without the other. God hath never made it the
> duty of some to take pains to teach those who are not obliged to
> take pains to learn.[2]

Not only can and should we learn in the church from the teachers God places there, but we can learn from all Christians within the church. Although just three chapters earlier Paul wrote of people in the church who were specially gifted by God to teach, in Romans 15:14 he says to the entire church body: "Now I myself am confident concerning you, my brethren, that you also are full of goodness, filled with all knowledge, able also to admonish one another." Haven't you ever learned from someone in the church who doesn't have nearly as much Bible knowledge or Christian experience as you but who has a different spiritual gift that enables him to see things you cannot? Haven't you learned from a newly converted Christian whose freshness and excitement for the things of God rebuked you for growing complacent spiritually? You have to learn in the church to experience these unexpected teachable moments from the Spirit of God through the family of God.

But while realizing that we can learn from everyone within the church, don't forget that God gives certain people within the church gifts to teach the rest of us. These people love to teach. They revel in the research beforehand. They thrive in the theological discussions afterward. They warn us of false teaching. They guide us in the things of God. They build up our souls. Teachers in the church are treasures from God, and we reject God's gifts if we don't learn in the church.

GOD'S GREATEST COMMANDMENT IS TO LOVE HIM WITH ALL YOUR MIND

What does God want most from you? Jesus answered that when someone asked Him, "What's the most important of all God's commandments?" In Mark 12:30 He replied, "You shall love the Lord your God with all your heart, with all your soul, with all your mind, and with all your strength." What God wants most is your love. More than sacrifice, more than obedience, and certainly more than money, God wants your love. For if He has your love, He has everything else.

But notice that one of the ways you show your love to God is by loving Him "with all your mind." Some professing Christians don't like that. They are willing, say, to love Him with all their strength. As indefatigable as ants, these folks will serve more faithfully than anyone else in the church. But they want to expend little *mental* energy loving God. And yet, to love God with every part of ourselves must include love from the head as well as from the heart and the hands.

Loving God with all your mind means loving Him with what you *mentally initiate*. Your mind is like a garden. The things you mentally initiate are the plants you purposefully put in your garden, the things that you go out of your way to bring into your mind. A wise person will turn to the place where Holy Scripture is proclaimed so that the truth of God will be planted in his mental furrows. Further, you can receive not only biblical teaching from godly men and women within the church, but also experienced counsel on seeding your mind with Christian biography, theology, spiritual classics, tapes, music, etc.

You also express love for God with your mind by what you *mentally cultivate*. Both weeds and good plants will grow in your thought-patch. If you want a successful garden you must learn to cultivate the right plants. Otherwise you'll have a tangled, overgrown confusion.

One way to till the right plants, that is, to develop the thoughts and thought-patterns that grow in God-loving ways, is to learn in a place that continually cultivates Godward thoughts. The church does that. The church teaches us: "Whatever things are true, whatever things are noble, whatever things are just, whatever things are pure, whatever things are lovely, whatever things are of good report, if there is any virtue and if there is anything praiseworthy—*meditate* on *these* things" (Philippians 4:8, italics added). If you aren't learning in the church you are certainly cultivating mental weeds that choke out love for God.

Third, you love God with your mind by what you *mentally tolerate*. You don't want to permit anything and everything that wanders or sneaks into the garden of your gray matter to remain. Just as you'd try to keep certain birds, rabbits, and other animals out of your backyard garden, so you shouldn't tolerate harmful things in your mind. You show your love for God by what you *refuse* to think about as well as by what you *do* think about. The truth of Scripture learned in the church will stand guard against those enemies that would ruin your garden. Nearly every week of my life God uses a word from His Word that I heard on Sunday to chase away thoughts that were not consistent with loving Him with all my mind. God wants us to devote our minds to things that increase the harvest of our love for Him, and learning in the church helps us do that.

LEARNING IN THE CHURCH
HELPS PROTECT YOU FROM ERRORS

I think it is a grave error to insist that individual Christians, guided by the Holy Spirit, cannot interpret Scripture for themselves. (Recall 1 John 2:27.) We are not dependent upon the church to tell us what the Bible means. But this is not the full picture. The balancing truth to this is that if we do not learn with the church we are likely to drift into erroneous, individualistic interpretations of Scripture. Increasingly we will find ourselves at odds with the established teaching of the Bible and more frequently objecting to others, "Well, that's *your* interpretation!"

Ultimately we can only speak for ourselves, so when we advocate the meaning of a particular verse of Scripture there is a sense in which such an accusation is always true. On the other hand, there is only one true interpretation of any passage, even though it may have countless applications. And in most verses in the Bible the meaning is unmistakably clear and there has been near unanimity in church history on it. Learning in the church tends to guide us better toward this meaning and steer us from an individualistic understanding of the passage.

This has been part of the ministry of the church since the beginning. In Acts 18:24–26 is an illustration of how a good man learned from the church and thereby became an even better servant of God.

> Now a certain Jew named Apollos, born at Alexandria, an eloquent man and mighty in the Scriptures, came to Ephesus. This man had been instructed in the way of the Lord; and being fervent in spirit, he spoke and taught accurately the things of the Lord, though he knew only the baptism of John. So he began to speak boldly in the synagogue. When Aquila and Priscilla heard him, they took him aside and explained to him the way of God more accurately.

Apollos "had been instructed in the way of the Lord" while in Alexandria. Moreover, surely through much additional study of his own, he became "mighty in the Scriptures." And yet, despite his brilliance, education, preaching experience, spiritual fervency, and personal efforts to grasp the truth, he still held an inaccurate understanding of some key matters related to "the way of God." Only when he was willing to learn from a couple in the church at Ephesus did he escape from the error he was inadvertently promoting. If someone as gifted and zealous as Apollos could misunderstand important doctrines without the teaching ministry of the church, so can we.

APPLYING WHAT YOU KNOW

Will you admit that you need *to learn in the church and that you* can *learn in the church?*

Will you participate in the most important way of learning in the church by listening to the preaching of God's Word?

Will you learn in the church by participating in a study group, such as a Sunday school class, discipleship class, Bible study, prayer group, etc.?

Will you begin now?

None of us has all insight, all understanding, or all spiritual gifts. As a result many of the terms, doctrines, meanings, and applications of Scripture may remain indecipherable without the "codebreakers" God has provided in the church. Are you wise enough and humble enough to learn from them?

CHAPTER THIRTEEN

WHY RESEARCH THE CHURCH?

. . . . ✤ . . . .

The decision you make about what church to
attend will greatly affect your spiritual life and
the lives of your children. In fact, the decisions you
make now will affect your descendants and the
generations to come. That's a sobering reality.

Mike Fitzhugh

Janet was born again when she was thirty-three. She encountered Christ through a study of God's Word with a handful of other women she had joined just a few months before. Once she came to know Christ she wanted to start going to church each Sunday.

Janet hadn't been to church since she was in high school, so she really didn't know what to look for in a church. But she had several reasons for attending the medium-sized congregation that she chose. A singer/songwriter, she was a regular performer in the folk music coffeehouse which entertained dozens each Friday night in the church basement. So besides feeling comfortable in the building, Janet's popularity in this well-known, weekly event meant she made friends with others who went to the church. Besides, her boyfriend claimed to be a Christian and was willing to go to this church, so she decided to go with him rather than attend where her Bible study friends worshiped.

The Word of God and the rich fellowship in her Bible study group nourished Janet's rapid growth in grace. At the same time, she began wrinkling her brow more and more frequently in confusion over things she heard at church. The turning point came in May when the pastor preached from John 20 and Jesus' appearance to Thomas and

187

the other disciples following His resurrection. He paused in his description of this story, leaned over the pulpit, and said, "Just between you and me, I don't think the disciples actually 'saw' Jesus. But I do think they had an experience of His presence."

Janet was appalled. "How could he say that?" she protested to her boyfriend.

"I think you misunderstood him," he said. So she made an appointment that week to talk with the pastor about it.

For an hour they discussed the miracles of Jesus. The minister denied each one, saying that the Bible's claims of the supernatural could be explained scientifically in every case. Dismayed, she asked her final question: "Well, what about Jesus' resurrection?"

"Oh, the resurrection," he said, standing up to signal the end of the interview. "I don't believe Jesus rose bodily. I believe it was a spiritual resurrection."

"I cried all the way home," Janet admitted to me, "and I never went back."

Do you have the discernment that would protect you from a dangerous church? Do you know how to research a church before you make it your church home?

Even if you are very happy with your present church family, the relocation rate in America points to the possibility that you will be moving to a new city and thus looking for a new church family in the not-too-distant future. Or, like Janet, you may have been unchurched and now are looking for a local assembly of believers for the first time. Or also as Janet did, the day may come for you when you must decide on another fellowship because your own church has fallen from biblical standards on crucial issues. For whatever reason you'll be searching, it's important to know how to find a new church since you almost certainly will have to do it—perhaps repeatedly.

So when you begin your search for a church to plant yourself in, here are some important things to remember:

RESEARCHING THE CHURCH WILL
HELP YOU AVOID AN UNFAITHFUL CHURCH

One reason it's important to conclude with a consideration of how to find a good church is that all the disciplines that have been addressed so far—attending, baptism, joining, listening to preaching, worshiping, witnessing, serving, giving, attending the ordinances, fellowshiping, praying, and learning—can be done in an unfaithful church. To avoid that, it is important to know what an unfaithful church looks like. Do you know the marks of a church that is disloyal to Christ and His Word?

In Revelation 2 and 3 Jesus Christ gives messages through the apostle John to seven specific churches that were located in what is now western Turkey. Two of these churches do not receive the kind of churchwide commendation that Christ gives to the other five. Worse, from the charges He brings against them it is obvious that they were untrue to Him. He describes one of these churches as "dead" and says to the other, "I will vomit you out of My mouth." Any church to whom Jesus Himself would say these things can surely be called an unfaithful church. From the characteristics of these churches we can learn to spot the kind of churches to avoid.

It Has Activities and Reputation Without Life

Jesus instructed John in Revelation 3:1, "And to the angel of the church in Sardis write, 'These things says He who has the seven Spirits of God and the seven stars: "I know your works, that you have a name that you are alive, but you are dead."'"

The church in Sardis had "works" and "a name," that is, activities and a reputation. People knew of the church as a group of nice people who did many good things. However, as the Puritan commentator, Matthew Henry, explained:

> This church was not really what it was reputed to be; they had a
> name to live, but they were dead; there was a form of godliness,
> but not the power; . . . if there was not a total privation of life, yet
> there was a great deadness in their souls, and in their services; a
> great deadness in the spirits of their ministers, and a great dead-
> ness in their ministr[ies], in their praying, in their preaching, in
> their convers[ations]; and a great deadness in the people in hear-
> ing, in prayer, and in conversation; what little life was yet left
> among them, was, in a manner, expiring, ready to die.[1]

Typically such assemblies once witnessed the transforming

power of Christ with regularity, thus the source of the "name" that they are alive. But now they are institutional and entirely predictable. The church and its worship services may run like clockwork—with about as much lifeblood. The church's flexibility to the Spirit and to ministry needs ossified, then became a mere shell of its previous ministries. Always referring to the glory of days past, few people realize that the real glory of the church has departed.

Dead churches are not necessarily devoid of activity, but of life. As you cannot judge a book by its cover, so you cannot judge a church by the number of programs and weekly activities it advertises. Although it's true that some dead churches are as motionless as a corpse, don't assume that a church is thriving simply because it can cram a calendar. Just as a decapitated chicken may run and writhe for a while, so a lot of vigorous activity in a church doesn't prove that it's alive spiritually.

It Never Accomplishes Anything for God

Christ also chided the church at Sardis in Revelation 3:2, "Be watchful, and strengthen the things which remain, that are ready to die, for I have not found your works perfect before God." Of course, no church's (and no individual's) works are sinlessly perfect before God. But the word translated *perfect* here in *The New King James Version* is from a Greek word that means to fill or complete. Thus the *New International* and *New American Standard* translations use the word *complete* or *completed* and quote Jesus as saying to this church, "I have not found your deeds *complete* in the sight of my God" (NIV, italics added). In short, the church's deeds were incomplete, inadequate.

Again, this church was busy, but there was something lacking in its busyness. As one commentator put it, "All of these religious activities were a failure because they were only formal and external, and not infused with the life-giving Holy Spirit."[2] The ministries of a church, no matter how impressive and glossy they appear, are incomplete "before God" without the power of the Spirit.

As a result, a Spirit-deficient, unfaithful church never really accomplishes anything of eternal significance. Like a beehive that produces no honey, such a church is busy but barren, failing to fulfill its purposes. Because the Spirit is not working through the people of the church, lives are not changed in the ways that Jesus changed them.

There's not much talk of people being saved, or even needing to be. People say more about self-fulfillment than laying down their lives to serve Christ. Concern for outsiders is always in reference to their temporal needs. The success of the church isn't measured by biblical standards or expressed in spiritual terms, but altogether in worldly fashion. Meeting the budget, a well-attended picnic, a winning softball team, a profitable bake or rummage sale—all things that may not be wrong in and of themselves, but are certainly peripheral to the church's purpose for existence—are touted week to week as the church's triumphs. Everything is explainable by hard work, new and more clever methodology, or sociological savvy. Nothing ever happens that can be accounted for only by the power of God.

It Has Forgotten the Scriptures and Faithful Preaching

Christ continues His rebuke of this unfaithful church in Revelation 3:3, "Remember therefore how you have received and heard; hold fast and repent." In effect He says, "You have received and heard the truth, but you have forgotten it." There had once been the sound preaching of God's truth in the church, but erosion of the message had occurred both in the pulpit and in the memories of the members.

When researching a church, notice how the Bible is referred to in Bible classes and in worship, but *especially* during the sermon. You can't always tell by one visit to the church or by one message, but if, after hearing the preacher several times, you observe a trend of the absence of Scripture, you have found a present-day church of Sardis.

A friend visited a church not long ago where during the entire message the pastor never opened the Bible or quoted from it. The closest he came was once when he used the word *love* and held up the Bible. I would hate to know how many churches endure such "preaching" on a weekly basis. Another friend told of being a guest teacher in an adult Sunday school class and discovering that not only had no one brought a Bible, but only a single, cover-torn copy of the Scriptures could be found throughout the building.

Conversely, what a delight it is to preach in a church where, as I announce my text, I hear pages being turned throughout the congregation. Invariably that signifies a church where the Word of God is still "received and heard." When pastor and people give attention to God's written revelation, their church rarely becomes an unfaithful church.

But if you visit a church where the Scriptures have been forgotten, forget that church.

It Is Indifferent to the Things of God

The other church Christ chastised as being unfaithful is the one at Laodicea. In Revelation 3:15–16 He warned, "I know your deeds, that you are neither cold nor hot. I wish you were either one or the other! So, because you are lukewarm—neither hot nor cold—I am about to spit you out of my mouth" (NIV). When Jesus Christ says, "Your church makes Me sick," that's a church you want to avoid.

Much as in a dead church, you can recognize a church that's lukewarm to the things of God by the general lack of conversation about spiritual matters. Prayers aren't vibrant with love for God. Preaching spawns yawns and nothing else. People seem dispassionate about matters regarding the kingdom of God. Few respond to opportunities—such as guest speakers, Bible studies, conferences, tapes, special events—that are intended primarily for building up the spiritual strength of the body (assuming the leadership offers them at all).

Caffy and I are good friends with a woman who grew up in a spiritually tepid church. Her parents still attend there, and when she and her husband go home to visit they go to church with their family. She recently described the church to me after returning from a visit earlier that day:

> From beginning to end, there is very little Scripture. If a place is given to Bible reading—something usually done by a layperson—it's done very irreverently. Either it's read in a sterile monotone or quickly and sing-songy with a slam of the cover shut at the end. I've never seen one person bring a Bible to church or pull out one of the Bibles from the back of a pew to follow along. The sermons aren't based on Scripture and nothing from Scripture is ever explained. . . . Some of the music was cutesy, and had absolutely nothing to do with God. Man is the focus, not God. . . . There's nothing really heretical; they just leave so much out.

To make matters worse, when a church is indifferent to the things of God, most people *don't care* that things are like this.

It Has No Sense of Need or of Dependence Upon God

Another criticism Jesus leveled at the Laodicean church was its sense of spiritual self-satisfaction. He expresses His displeasure this way in Revelation 3:17, "You say, 'I am rich, have become wealthy, and have need of nothing'—and do not know that you are wretched, miserable, poor, blind, and naked." This church was content with material wealth but unaware of its abject spiritual poverty. The abundant provision for their bodies made them overlook the necessities of their souls.

The words of Jesus to His disciples, "Without Me you can do nothing" (John 15:5), apply to entire churches as well. If you visit a church that operates as though it never heard this, remember that no matter how well-manicured its grounds and well-appointed its buildings, it is nauseating to Christ and should be to you as well.

Take care if the spirit of a church seems to be "Our attendance is strong, giving is good, our property is in a prime location, the buildings are attractive, we have a dynamic pastor, and we have enough money in the bank to get through almost any crisis—what more could we possibly need?" All of these things are desirable, but if you are considering attending such a church, make sure it doesn't depend upon these things more than upon God. And if the church can forecast its future in great detail, such as telling how many people it will add or see converted in a given time because of its giftedness, strategy, etc., realize that it is not trusting in grace. Look and listen for ways that the church is asking God to do what He *alone* can do.

Unfaithful churches can have a numbing effect on even the best Christians among those who join them. They can turn the spiritually zealous into spiritual zombies. I've seen strong believers leave a good church, move to another area and join an unfaithful church, then soon find themselves almost mindlessly going through the motions of Christianity. All the while their souls are starving. Some transfer and think they can single-handedly bring reformation to such unfaithful churches. But rarely does a single hot coal ignite the rest; usually the mass of cooler ones prevails. Research the church carefully. Unfaithful churches don't build faithful Christians.

RESEARCHING THE CHURCH WILL
HELP YOU AVOID AN UNFAITHFUL MINISTER

Unfaithful churches and unfaithful ministers tend to be found together. However, there are exceptions. For example, it is possible to find a church that has been generally faithful but now has an unfaithful minister. The discovery of this may lead to the pastor's departure. On the other hand, he may manage to deceive the church well enough to maintain his position, then stay there for years and gradually lead the church into unfaithfulness to Christ and His Word. Though you may see no other feasible option for the immediate future than to join a faithful church despite its unfaithful minister, make sure that you know how to discern a dangerous man in a devoted church.

The New Testament Repeatedly Warns Us to Watch Out for False Prophets

Almost every book in the New Testament—22 of the 27—gives at least one warning about false prophets, that is, those who teach error.[3]
Note the serious, urgent tone of these repeated warnings:

- Beware of false prophets, who come to you in sheep's clothing, but inwardly they are ravenous wolves. (Matthew 7:15)

- Take heed to yourselves and to all the flock, among which the Holy Spirit has made you overseers, to shepherd the church of God which He purchased with His own blood. For I know this, that after my departure savage wolves will come in among you, not sparing the flock. Also from among yourselves men will rise up, speaking perverse things, to draw away the disciples after themselves. (Acts 20:28–30)

- But there were also false prophets among the people, even as there will be false teachers among you, who will secretly bring in destructive heresies. (2 Peter 2:1)

- Beloved, do not believe every spirit, but test the spirits, whether they are of God; because many false prophets have gone out into the world. (1 John 4:1)

Those who are the most dangerous don't look dangerous. They

are wolves, "ravenous" and "savage," but they are difficult to identify as such because they are in "sheep's clothing." Their outward appearance and interpersonal skills rarely show them up as betrayers of the Scriptures. You should learn to recognize them, or you could become one of those whom they "draw away."

The Presence of Many False Prophets Is a Sign of Jesus' Return

One of the reasons the New Testament warns so frequently about spiritual predators is that they lurk everywhere. The apostle John sounds the alert: "For *many* deceivers have gone out into the world who do not confess Jesus Christ as coming in the flesh" (2 John 7, italics added). One type of deceiver is the minister who does not believe that Jesus was fully human or teaches that His resurrection was only a spiritual one, not bodily. According to this verse, there are "many deceivers" of this type alone, not to mention others.

Interestingly, Jesus said that one of the signs foreshadowing His return would be the rise of *many* false prophets: "Then many false prophets will rise up and deceive many" (Matthew 24:11). But while we can expect a rise in the number of false prophets prior to the Lord's return, we mustn't forget that John emphasized there will *always* be many who will lead people from the truth.

Don't overreact to this warning by being suspicious of every minister. There are also many good and godly ones. The plethora of New Testament cautions, combined with TV and Hollywood's portrayals of clergymen, may give you the impression that nearly all ministers are crooks or kooks. That's not so. On the other hand, don't be naive and assume that just because a man is in the ministry, pastors a church, has a media ministry, or publishes material that he is doctrinally sound.

Some Men Disqualify Themselves by Becoming Unfaithful to Biblical Standards

A church should evaluate a man by the requirements of 1 Timothy 3:2–6 before it calls him as pastor.

> A bishop [a word used synonymously in the New Testament with "elder" and "pastor"] then must be blameless, the husband of one wife, temperate, sober-minded, of good behavior, hospitable, able

to teach; not given to wine, not violent, not greedy for money, but gentle, not quarrelsome, not covetous; one who rules his own house well, having his children in submission with all reverence (for if a man does not know how to rule his own house, how will he take care of the church of God?); not a novice, lest being puffed up with pride he fall into the same condemnation as the devil.

However, it is not only possible that a church you are considering could call a man even though his life was in violation of these criteria, but sometimes men who *begin* faithfully will transgress these standards *during* their pastorate. No man always measures up to all aspects of this list perfectly. But obvious failures to live according to the biblical requirements for a pastor disqualify a man from being your minister. And how will you know these things unless, in a suitable way and with the right spirit, you observe and inquire?

Some Hearers Will Find Men to Preach to Their Felt Needs

Paul warned Timothy that some people would have a propensity toward false teachers. Unable to endure convicting, doctrinal preaching anymore, they will find men who will preach to their felt needs or be more entertaining.

"For the time will come," Paul warns, "when they will not endure sound doctrine, but according to their own desires, because they have itching ears, they will heap up for themselves teachers; and they will turn their ears away from the truth, and be turned aside to fables" (2 Timothy 4:3–4). Research an assembly before you join to make sure that you do not slip into a sinkhole of a church that has just the kind of pied-piper storytelling its ears itch for.

Shun a church that wants or allows preaching to be minimized. Steer clear of a preacher who sounds as though he models his delivery after the style of stand-up comics or late-night TV entertainers. Be wary of a pastor who spends most of his sermon time telling stories. Some argue that since much of Jesus' teaching was by means of parables then preachers today should maximize the use of stories to communicate biblical truth. Obviously Jesus did tell many parables. But there is a difference between divinely inspired parables told by the Son of God and a preacher's stories. The job of the preacher today isn't to tell stories as Jesus did, but to tell and explain the stories *of* Jesus, that is, the stories about Him as well as the ones He told. The recorded sermons of the apostles aren't a series of stories strung together like beads on a string. Speaking through Paul, God has commanded preachers, "Preach the word!" (2 Timothy 4:2), not merely tell stories that illustrate the Word. I am not arguing against the appropriate use of illustrations to clarify and apply the truths of Scripture. What I want to protect you against is just the opposite, namely the man who seems to use Scripture for little more than clarifying and applying his stories.

In *Selling Jesus: What's Wrong with Marketing the Church,* Douglas Webster elaborates,

> There are so many illustrations in today's market-sensitive sermons that the hearer forgets the biblical truth that is being illustrated; so many personal anecdotes that the hearer knows the pastor better than she knows Christ; . . . No wonder nominal Christians leave church feeling upbeat. Their self-esteem is safely intact. Their minds and hearts have been sparked and soothed with sound-bite theology, Christian maxims and a few practical pointers dealing with self-esteem, kids or work. But the question remains: has the Word of God been effectively and faithfully proclaimed, penetrating comfort zones and the veneer of self-satisfaction with the truth of Jesus Christ?[4]

HOW CAN WE IDENTIFY FALSE TEACHERS?

The most concentrated section in the Bible on this subject is in the second chapter of the apostle Peter's second letter. The first nineteen verses reveal at least nineteen insights into the character and methods you may find in these impersonators of godliness. Some of these include:

- They don't tell you openly that they are teaching things that are contrary to historic, orthodox doctrine; rather, they "secretly bring in destructive heresies" (v. 1).

- They will occasionally be heard, perhaps privately more than publicly, "denying the Lord" in various ways (v. 1).

- They "will exploit you" if necessary, through various means of manipulation, in order to get from you what they need to satisfy their covetousness (v. 3).

- They covertly indulge their immoral sexual appetites, most likely with pornography and illicit sex, as they "walk according to the flesh in the lust of uncleanness" (v. 10).

- They must be the boss and have the last word because they "despise authority" (v. 10).

- They often act on their own and without counsel (or in spite of it), for they are "presumptuous" (v. 10).

- They frequently disregard the wishes or privileges of others because they are "self-willed," usually to the point of being arrogant (v. 10).

- They may mock Satan and his demons or even scoff at the possibility of their existence, for "they are not afraid to speak evil of dignitaries" [which, in the context, seems to refer to evil angels] (v. 10).

- They know little of the Bible since they really don't study it much, and yet they "speak evil of the things they do not understand" (v. 12).

- They have "eyes full of adultery and that cannot cease from sin," and are always looking lustfully at women, always on the lookout for a woman who would commit adultery with them (v. 14).

- They are skilled at "enticing unstable souls," luring them into error, into giving money and support, and/or into immorality (v. 14).

- They may be powerful religious orators, but they say nothing of lasting spiritual value, for "they speak great swelling words of emptiness" (v. 18).

- They are, however, despite all their promises to others, "them-selves . . . slaves of corruption," not experiencing what they are teaching (v. 19).

By failing to research the church you become interested in, you could unwittingly place yourself under the teaching of such a man. The consequences to you and your family could be devastating.

A faithful British minister of the 1800s saw this danger and wrote, "I warn everyone who loves his soul to be jealous as to the preaching he regularly hears and the place of worship he regularly attends. He who deliberately settles down under a ministry which is unsound is a very unwise man. If false doctrine is preached in a church a man who loves his soul is not right in going to that church."[5]

HOW SHOULD YOU RESEARCH THE CHURCH YOU CONSIDER JOINING?

Let me make some suggestions on the process of determining whether a particular church is the one in which you should invest yourself.

Discover What the Church (and Especially the Pastor) Believes

In an article on "Finding the Right Church," Jeanette Gardner noted, "When you're seriously considering a new church, don't hesi-tate to set up an appointment with the pastor, staff member, or other leader. If you don't ask questions, you can't expect to have them answered."[6] It is through asking questions that you learn where the church and the pastor stand.

Sometimes new Christians believe that almost any organization with "church" in its name will have orthodox preaching, offer Bible studies, be God-centered, and hold to certain historic fundamentals of the faith. Remember from the introduction of this chapter how shocked Janet was to discover that her pastor did not believe in the bodily resurrection of Jesus? Of course, basic, universal orthodoxy has never been true, but today you can't assume anything about a church, not even by its denominational label (if the church has one). I have a newspaper clipping in my files of a pastor who says she does not believe in God! Wouldn't you think that at least one thing you could take for granted about someone with the title of "pastor" is that she *wouldn't* be an *atheist*?

Pastors with such heretical views surely represent a tiny percentage of the clergy, but this example shows you can be sure of very little anymore by the words *church* or *pastor*. So it is imperative to ask questions to learn what the pastor and church believe.

A few years ago a couple from our church was transferred to another part of the country. As one of my last pastoral ministries to them, I wanted to help them find a good church home in their new location. However, they were young in the faith and I knew that they might not be ready to discern a spiritual wolf in a pastor's clothing. So I quickly jotted down for them a list of questions to ask a prospective pastor. They found the questions helpful, as did others for whom I expanded the list and made copies as they moved away. Perhaps you can benefit by asking some of these questions the next time you are looking for a church home.

Keep in mind the following tips when using the questions:

Ask wisely. Talk to the pastor if at all possible. If not, then ask another staff member of the church.

Ask personally. Visit or call him. Do not mail, fax, or E-mail these and ask for a written reply.

Ask courteously. Do not "grill" the pastor or ask aggressively.

Ask selectively. Do not ask all these questions at one time. The more serious you become about membership, the more appropriate it becomes to ask additional questions later.

These questions are not necessarily listed in the order of significance. Some of them may not be important to you. You may want to add others.

- How is a person made right with God?

- What is your position on the inerrancy of Scripture?

- Do you believe Genesis 1–11 is historical or symbolic?

- Do you believe that Jesus Christ is the only way to heaven?

- What is your position on the Lordship Salvation issue? Can a person take Jesus as Savior without taking Him as Lord?

- Do you believe that Jesus Christ was born of a virgin?

- Do you believe in the bodily return of Jesus Christ?

- Do you believe in a literal hell?

- What is your position on the ordination of women for positions of church leadership?

- How do you deal with a young child who says he or she wants to be saved? (Of interest to parents)

- How do you combat easy-believism?

- What are your views regarding divorce and remarriage?

- What is your position on the Charismatic Movement?

- How would you/the church handle a case of scandal or immorality by a church member?

- What is your position on church debt? Is the church in debt?

- Have there been any splits in the church, or have any pastors been asked to leave?

- What have been the high points (or the best thing) in this church in the last five years? In the last six months?

- What are the greatest strengths of this church? Weaknesses?

- What do you think is your greatest ministry strength? Weakness?

- How do you foster the spiritual growth of individuals in your church?

- What are your goals for the church?

- Would you mind telling me about your devotional life?

- Who are your favorite authors?

- What is the doctrinal statement of the church, and may I have a copy? (Note: be cautious if the church has no doctrinal statement or cannot find a copy.)

- Does the church follow its constitution and by-laws, and may I have a copy?

- Does a large percentage of the church differ with your position on any of these issues?

A pastor does not have to have full and ready answers to all these questions in order to be a good and faithful minister. Realize that with some of these questions it is acceptable for him to say, "I don't know" or "I don't have my position completely developed on that yet."

However, beware a pastor who will not give clear answers. Certainly with many questions he may find it necessary to define terms and qualify his response. But having done so, proceed carefully if he still seems to avoid making his positions plain.

Also watch out for the minister who refuses to hear your questions at all. One pastor who saw this list became angry with me. He said if someone ever asked such questions of him that he would have no time for them. His reason? They should trust him and the church. He wrote that it was inappropriate for him to answer prospective members' questions because, "*I* would not be joining *them*, *they* would be joining *us*." Whereas applying for church membership is a two-way street in that the pastor also has the responsibility to ask some questions (e.g., about the genuineness of the conversion) of those who apply for membership, be suspicious of a pastor who is offended by your inquiries. How can you support and follow a man when you don't know what he believes and where he's going?

Discover What the Church Does

You can learn a lot about a church by observing what ministries it has and the things it promotes. For instance, does the church offer opportunities to learn what God has to say to us through His Word? Is the church concerned about outreach? What about ministries to children, teenagers, singles, mothers of preschoolers, senior adults, or other groups of particular interest to you? Many good churches do not have ministries to a wide variety of groups. But often you can determine the strengths and direction of a church by its ministry priorities.

Here's where to look for these things, provided the church has each of the following:

- the visitor's brochure
- the bulletin or worship folder
- the church newsletter
- the bulletin board
- the church's home page on the Internet

Another way to find out what the church does is to ask several people, "What ministries are most important to this church?" and "What does this church do best?"

Discover Who the People Are

This requires two things: time and attendance. Jeffrey Dennis makes this point in his article "How to Find a New Church Home": "When you walk into the church for the first time, don't look for an 'at-home feeling' or a sense of being welcomed by the congregation. Few people feel at home in strange places, or particularly welcomed by a group of strangers."[7]

Once you have some of your preliminary questions settled, attend the church for a while and find ways to be around the people informally. Go to small group meetings if possible, such as Sunday school or Bible study classes, fellowship groups, churchwide social activities, etc. Although you can learn a lot by watching to see if everyone leaves immediately after church or if many linger and visit, you simply can't get to know the members of the church in one or two visits to a worship service.

There's more to finding a good church than one with the right answers and right doctrine. British pastor Daniel Wray strikes the balance between spirit and truth in a church:

> You are duty-bound not to affiliate with any church which denies any of the fundamental doctrines of the Christian faith; . . . The churches of Christ are clearly responsible to uphold God's truth; therefore this is a vital criterion when choosing a church (see 1 Tim. 3:15; 2 Tim. 1:13, 14, 2:2; Jude 3). A true church will place a strong emphasis on the importance of truth.
>
> On the other hand, let us remember that love for the truth

should not exist in isolation from love for people, especially those of the household of faith (Gal. 6:10). Sometimes one will encounter churches which are strict in their adherence to theological orthodoxy, while neglecting love and works of evangelism and mercy. . . . Seek a church which is trying to practise all of these virtues together. We should be as zealous for love and mercy as we are for truth, and *vice versa.*[8]

Do the people of the church love the church? Do they like to be together? Do they socialize together outside the walls of the church building? Do many of them appear to be growing spiritually? Do they frequently backbite and criticize each other and the pastor? Do many participate in the ministries of the church, or do nearly all attend just once a week? Look and listen, for these people will become your local spiritual family.

MORE APPLICATION

The ideal church may not exist—at least not in your area.

You probably cannot find a church or a pastor that will answer *all* your questions to your satisfaction. It's unrealistic to think that you will locate a church with all the programs and ministries you've hoped for, with just the right number of people, in just the right location, with just the right style of worship, with just the right spirit, and with just the right pastor.

One writer reminds us: "We must be careful not to get so picky that we abuse the options we have, and begin to taint our perspective of what a church is to be about. . . . We, too, have a responsibility to God, to our fellow Christians and to ourselves not to become so demanding that no church will ever truly satisfy our desires."[9]

Don't run from church to church trying to find one exactly like the one you loved in another town or in another time. You won't find it. Each church is unique. Ultimately you may have to ask yourself, "Can I live with the things I don't like about this church?" And if you did recently relocate and leave a wonderful church home behind, remember that you probably didn't love that church as much when you first joined it as you did when you had to move. You can expect the same to be true with your new church family.

A good church is worth a good distance.

Good churches can be so rare that, when you find one, distance alone (unless it is unreasonable) shouldn't keep you from it. You may be accustomed to traveling only a short distance to church. If so, don't limit your new church search to the same travel time or less. Don't exchange a faithful church for a convenient one. It's better to have a good church in a bad location than a bad church in a good location.

I baptized a woman who grew to be very dear to Caffy and me. At the time of her conversion her husband was not a Christian and she had to drive to church on her own. Soon after her baptism I noticed her absence more and more frequently. When I spoke with her about it she said she had been visiting another church. I asked if there was a problem with her relationship with our church. She said, "No. That church is only two minutes from home and this one is just too far." She has often reminded me that I blurted out, "Too *far?*" I was comparing her ten-minute drive across town to the thirty- and forty-minute drives some were making, and I reacted reflexively. But she had never had to travel more than five minutes to church and ten minutes seemed too far. It wasn't long before she realized that the church she had been visiting was not the place she needed to be, and that an extra eight to ten minutes each way was worth the difference.

Another couple married and moved to a city of several million people. Both knew the value of a good church and were willing to drive as much as thirty minutes in any direction to find a church with good preaching, worship, and fellowship. They were open to a wide variety of denominations as well as independent churches. You would think that in any American city of multiple millions you could randomly put your finger at any spot on the city map and find a good church in a circle with a one-hour driving diameter across it. They told me that they made phone calls and visits for months. Finally, though it meant a much longer commute to work for the husband, they decided that for their spiritual health they had to move to another part of the metropolitan area where they knew of a good church. I am not willing to say that there is not one tolerable evangelical church in that part of that city. But I do know that you should consider yourself blessed if you have more than one acceptable church choice available to you. If the only good church is far away, for the sake of your soul, do what it takes to get there.

The Lord wants you to find a church where you can be involved.

Despite all the unfaithful churches in your area and the many negative things you can say about even the best churches around, the fact remains that you need a church. We can't use the unfaithfulness of churches as excuses for disobedience to the command about not forsaking the assembling of ourselves together (Hebrews 10:25). Don't look for a church indefinitely. Don't visit the "cycle" of prospective churches over and over. Prayerfully, but decisively, choose a church and, despite its shortcomings, do all you can to help the work of Jesus Christ prosper there.

If all the churches in your vicinity are unbiblical, consider helping to start a new one.

I have visited in towns where I asked myself, "The church situation here is so terrible, if I lived here, what would I do?" Maybe that's the kind of place where you *do* live. Perhaps you've never thought of it before, but consider the possibility of being part of a new church start.

If you are presently a member of a local church there, talk with your pastor. Ask if he has given any thought to the church sponsoring a new work in town. If so, your interest in starting a new church may be the answer to his prayers. If he is not enthusiastic about the idea, or if you are not yet a member of a church in the area, talk to a local official of your denomination (provided you have a denominational affiliation). This may mean someone with a title such as director of missions, bishop, or missionary, depending upon the denomination. Most denominations are always interested in helping new churches to start. They may even know of others who have expressed a similar interest. Having the support, prayers, counsel, and resources of another local church or group of churches from the outset is more important than you may yet be able to appreciate.

I knew a couple who had moved several times during their marriage, but had come to love their present church home far more than any other they'd ever been in. After more than a decade in this church the husband was offered a promotion which meant relocating. As the couple discussed the possibility with me, they listed the benefits: reducing the commute to work from thirty minutes to five; getting their children away from unsatisfactory schools and troublesome friends; living in a much smaller and slower-paced city; residing in an area with a dramatically lower cost of living; increasing their income; and having the opportunity to buy their dream home debt free with the equity from the sale of their present house.

My question was, "Do you know you can find a good church there?"

"No," said the wife, "but we know there are many churches in town. Surely at least one of them is a good one."

"You know how often you have said that your current church is the best one of your lives. Are you willing to risk that for these other things?" I probed.

Within weeks they were in their beautiful new home, enjoying the new job, new town, new schools, etc. And while they eventually settled—somewhat reluctantly—into a new church, they spoke of how discouraged they were by it and how that occasionally they were so grieved by something in a service that they had to walk out and go home. In a few months they told me that they regretted ever leaving their former church. All the changes for which they made the move lost their brilliance in the shadow of an unhappy church life. Previously the blessings of an encouraging church helped them endure the discouraging parts of their lives. However, following the move they discovered that the many positive changes they enjoyed could not fill the strange, withering leanness in their souls, a leanness they had to endure for years.

They are now part of a core group trying to start a new work. If your church research forecasts a spiritual famine for you if current conditions continue, that may be the Lord's way of prompting you to help plant a new church.

The opening quotation for this chapter is worth repeating at the conclusion as a reminder of the cruciality of carefully researching any church you consider joining: "The decision you make about what church to attend will greatly affect your spiritual life and the lives of your children. In fact, the decisions you make now will affect your descendants and the generations to come."[10]

NOTES

·······✦·······

CHAPTER ONE

1. George Barna, *What Americans Believe* (Ventura, Calif.: Regal, 1991), 245.
2. George Barna, *The Barna Report: 1992–93* (Ventura, Calif.: Regal, 1992), 54.
3. Barna, *What Americans Believe,* 249–50.
4. Paul R. Van Gorder, "Why Go to Church?" *Our Daily Bread,* 15 October 1989.
5. Kenneth Kantzer, "Alone with God Is Not Enough," *Christianity Today,* 9 March 1992, 19.

CHAPTER TWO

1. Gary Mihoces, "For 'Super Fans,' It's Not Just a Game," *USA Today,* 25 November 1994.
2. Erroll Hulse, *The Testimony of Baptism* (Haywards Heath, England: Carey, 1982), 16–17.
3. Matthew Henry, *A Commentary on the Whole Bible,* vol. 5 (New York: Funk and Wagnalls, n.d.), 257.

CHAPTER THREE

1. C. K. Barrett, *A Commentary on the First Epistle to the Corinthians* (New York: Harper & Row, 1968), 324.
2. Joseph Hall, as quoted in John Blanchard, comp., *More Gathered Gold* (Welwyn, England: Evangelical Press, 1986), 43.
3. G. Eric Lane, *I Want to Be a Church Member* (Bryntirion, Wales: Evangelical Press of Wales, 1992), 21.
4. Douglas G. Millar, "Should I Join a Church?" *The Banner of Truth,* no. 62 (November 1968), 21.
5. John F. MacArthur, Jr., "Commitment to the Church" Tape GC 80–130 (Panorama City, Calif.: Grace to You, 1994).
6. Ibid.
7. Ben Patterson, "Why Join a Church?" *Leadership,* Fall Quarter, 1984, 80.
8. MacArthur, "Commitment to the Church."
9. D. Martyn Lloyd-Jones, *Knowing the Times* (Edinburgh: The Banner of Truth Trust, 1989), 30.

CHAPTER FOUR

1. J. I. Packer in Samuel T. Logan, Jr., ed., *The Preacher and Preaching: Reviving the Art in the Twentieth Century* (Phillipsburg, N.J.: Presbyterian and Reformed, 1986), 15.
2. Eric J. Alexander, *Plainly Teaching the Word: Messages on Expository Preaching* (Thornhill, Ontario: Bayview Glen Church, n.d.), 9.
3. C. H. Spurgeon, "Hearing with Heed," in *Metropolitan Tabernacle Pulpit* (London: Passmore and Alabaster, 1898; reprint, Pasadena, Tex.: Pilgrim Publications, 1976), vol. 43, 178.

4. David Clarkson, *The Works of David Clarkson* (London: James Nichol, 1864; reprint ed., Edinburgh: The Banner of Truth Trust, 1988), vol. 3, 193–94.
5. J. I. Packer in *The Preacher and Preaching: Reviving the Art in the Twentieth Century* (Phillipsburg, N.J.: Presbyterian and Reformed, 1986), 20.
6. Martin Luther, as quoted in John Blanchard, comp., *Gathered Gold* (Welwyn, England: Evangelical Press, 1984), 238.
7. W. Herschel Ford, *Simple Sermons on Prayer* (Grand Rapids: Zondervan, 1969), 34.
8. Eric W. Hayden, *Highlights in the Life of Charles Haddon Spurgeon* (Pasadena, Tex.: Pilgrim Publications, 1990), 49.

CHAPTER FIVE

1. C. H. Spurgeon, "Serving the Lord with Gladness," in *Metropolitan Tabernacle Pulpit* (London: Passmore and Alabaster, 1868; reprint, Pasadena, Tex.: Pilgrim Publications, 1989), vol. 13, 500.
2. Geoffrey Thomas, "Worship in Spirit," *The Banner of Truth,* August-September 1987, 8.
3. Matthew Henry, *A Commentary on the Bible* (New York: Funk and Wagnalls, n.d.), vol. 3, 339.
4. John Blanchard, comp., *Gathered Gold* (Welwyn, Hertfordshire, England: Evangelical Press, 1984), 342.
5. David Clarkson, *The Works of David Clarkson* (London: James Nichol, 1864; reprint, Edinburgh, Scotland: The Banner of Truth Trust, 1988), vol. 3, 206.

CHAPTER SIX

1. Francis Schaeffer, *The Mark of the Christian,* The Complete Works of Francis Schaeffer: A Christian Worldview, Vol. 4, *A Christian View of the Church* (Westchester, Ill.: Crossway, 1982), 190.
2. Will Metzger, *Tell the Truth* (Downers Grove, Ill.: InterVarsity, 1984), 2d ed., 157.
3. Tertullian, *Apology,* reprint ed., eds. Alexander Roberts and James Donaldson, The Ante-Nicene Fathers (Grand Rapids: Eerdmans, 1986), 3:46.
4. Metzger, *Tell the Truth,* 157.
5. Ibid.

CHAPTER SEVEN

1. "A Service of Love," *Our Daily Bread,* 28 June 1986.
2. C. H. Spurgeon, "Weak Hands and Feeble Knees," in *New Park Street Pulpit* (Passmore and Alabaster, 1861; reprint, Pasadena, Tex.: Pilgrim Publications, 1981), vol. 5, 146.
3. C. H. Spurgeon, *Words of Counsel for Christian Workers* (Pasadena, Tex.: Pilgrim Publications, 1985), 57.
4. Stephen A. Bly, "Are We Having Fun Yet?" *Moody,* June 1992, 17.
5. Gordon W. Prange, *At Dawn We Slept* (Middlesex, England: Penguin, 1981), 737–38.

CHAPTER EIGHT

1. Gene A. Getz, *A Biblical Theology of Material Possessions* (Chicago: Moody, 1990), 109.

2. Richard B. Cunningham, "Principles and Procedures of Responsible Giving," *Resource Unlimited,* ed. William L. Hendricks, (Nashville: The Stewardship Commission of the Southern Baptist Convention, 1972), 233.
3. Ibid., 229.
4. Getz, *Biblical Theology of Material Possessions,* 232.
5. "Americans Giving Less at Church, Study Says," *Chicago Tribune,* 9 December 1994.
6. Quoted in "Americans Don't Connect Faith, Finances," *The Illinois Baptist,* 22 December 1993.
7. Quoted in *How to Manage Your Money,* 15 September 1990.

CHAPTER NINE

1. John MacArthur, Jr. and the Master's Seminary Faculty, *Rediscovering Pastoral Ministry* (Dallas: Word, 1995), 351.
2. David S. Dockery, "The Lord's Supper in the New Testament and in Baptist Worship," *Search,* Fall 1988, 40.
3. John Calvin, *Institutes of the Christian Religion,* ed. John T. McNeil, trans. and indexed by Ford Lewis Battles, (Philadelphia: Westminster, 1960), vol. 2, 1403.
4. Charles Hodge, *A Commentary on 1 & 2 Corinthians* (1857; reprint, Edinburgh: The Banner of Truth Trust, 1 vol. ed., 1974), 229–30.

CHAPTER TEN

1. *Theological Dictionary of the New Testament,* ed. Gerhard Kittel and Gerhard Friedrich, trans. Geoffrey W. Bromiley, abridged in 1 vol. (Grand Rapids: Eerdmans, 1985), 448–49.
2. John MacArthur, Jr., *The Church: The Body of Christ,* edited and outlined by David Sper (Panorama City, Calif.: Word of Grace Communications, 1981), 51.
3. J. I. Packer, "Body Life," *Tenth,* July 1981, 11:3, 63. (Privately printed.)
4. Donald S. Whitney, *Spiritual Disciplines for the Christian Life* (Colorado Springs: NavPress, 1991), 230.
5. Maurice Roberts, "The Fellowship of Saints," *The Banner of Truth,* June, 1989, 1.
6. Packer, "Body Life," 63.
7. John Owen, *Works,* vol. 9, (London: Johnstone and Hunter, 1850–53; reprint ed., Edinburgh: The Banner of Truth Trust, 1965), 267.
8. Iain Murray, *Jonathan Edwards: A New Biography* (Edinburgh: The Banner of Truth Trust, 1987), 406.
9. Jerry Bridges, *True Fellowship* (Colorado Springs: NavPress, 1985), 76.
10. Packer, "Body Life," 64.
11. John Wesley, as quoted by J. I. Packer in *God's Words: Studies of Key Bible Themes* (Downers Grove, Ill.: InterVarsity, 1981), 199.
12. For a description of this meeting, see Iain Murray, *David Martyn Lloyd-Jones: The Fight of Faith 1939–1981* (Edinburgh: The Banner of Truth Trust, 1990), 167–75.
13. Alister E. McGrath, *Spirituality in an Age of Change* (Grand Rapids: Zondervan, 1994), 120.

CHAPTER ELEVEN

1. George Barna, *Absolute Confusion: The Barna Report,* vol. 3 (Ventura, Calif.: Regal, 1993), 93–94.

2. Gene A. Getz, *Praying for One Another* (Wheaton, Ill.: Victor, 1982), 11–12.
3. E. M. Bounds, *The Complete Works of E. M. Bounds on Prayer* (Grand Rapids: Baker, 1990), 75.
4. Bounds, *Complete Works,* 134.
5. T. W. Hunt and Catherine Walker, *PrayerLife* (Nashville: The Sunday School Board of the Southern Baptist Convention, 1988), 103.
6. T. W. Hunt, *The Doctrine of Prayer* (Nashville: Convention Press, 1986), 108.
7. Bounds, *The Complete Works,* 487.
8. Samuel Prime, *The Power of Prayer* (1859; reprint ed., Edinburgh: The Banner of Truth Trust, 1991), 255.
9. Owen Murphy, "When God Stepped Down from Heaven: Revival in the Scottish Hebrides 1949–1952," *Revival: The Need of the Times,* Jan./Feb. 1994, 8–9.
10. Erroll Hulse, "Global Revival: Should We Be Involved in Concerts of Prayer?" *Reformation and Revival Journal,* vol. 2, no. 4, Fall 1993, 52.
11. Leslie K. Tarr, "A Prayer Meeting That Lasted 100 Years," *Christian History,* vol. I, no. 1, 18.
12. Erroll Hulse, "Global Revival," 81.
13. Andrew Murray, *With Christ in the School of Prayer* (Old Tappan, N.J.: Revell, 1953), 83.
14. John Flavel, *Works,* vol. 2 (W. Bayns and Son, 1820; reprint ed., Edinburgh: The Banner of Truth Trust, 1968), 266.

CHAPTER TWELVE

1. "Codebreakers," a *Nova* program produced by WGBH, Boston, and aired on Public Television, January 1994.
2. Jonathan Edwards, "Christian Knowledge," *Works,* vol. 2 (reprint ed., Edinburgh: Banner of Truth Trust, 1986), 161.

CHAPTER THIRTEEN

1. Matthew Henry, *A Commentary on the Holy Bible* (New York: Funk and Wagnalls, n.d.), vol. 6, 1384.
2. George Eldon Ladd, *A Commentary on the Revelation of John* (Grand Rapids: Eerdmans, 1972), 56.
3. See Matthew 7:15; Mark 13:22; Luke 21:8; Acts 20:28-30; Romans 16:17–18; 1 Corinthians 16:13; 2 Corinthians 11:13–15; Galatians 2:4; Ephesians 4:14; Philippians 3:2; Colossians 2:8; 2 Thessalonians 2:3; 1 Timothy 1:4–7; 2 Timothy 2:14–18; Titus 3:9; Hebrews 13:9; 2 Peter 2:1; 1 John 4:1; 2 John 10; 3 John 10; Jude 4; Revelation 2:2.
4. Douglas D. Webster, *Selling Jesus: What's Wrong with Marketing the Church* (Downers Grove, Ill.: InterVarsity, 1992), 83–84.
5. J. C. Ryle, as quoted in *Evangelical Times,* July 1994, 14.
6. Jeanette D. Gardner, "Finding the Right Church," *Moody,* June 1994, 39.
7. Jeffrey P. Dennis, "How to Find a New Church Home," *Discipleship Journal,* issue 66, 1991, 18.
8. Daniel Wray, *The Importance of the Local Church* (Edinburgh: The Banner of Truth Trust, 1981), 14.
9. George Barna, *Finding a Church You Can Call Home* (Ventura, Calif.: Regal, 1992), 141.
10. Mike Fitzhugh, "What to Look for When Choosing a New Church Home," *Masterpiece,* July/August 1990, 13.

SCRIPTURE INDEX